BROADMOOR

BROADMOOR

James B. Weaver
And
Larry G. Weaver

iUniverse, Inc.
New York Lincoln Shanghai

BROADMOOR

All Rights Reserved © 2003 by James B. Weaver and Larry G. Weaver

No part of this book may be reproduced or transmitted in any form or by any means, graphic, electronic, or mechanical, including photocopying, recording, taping, or by any information storage retrieval system, without the written permission of the publisher.

iUniverse, Inc.

For information address:
iUniverse, Inc.
2021 Pine Lake Road, Suite 100
Lincoln, NE 68512
www.iuniverse.com

ISBN: 0-595-29127-9 (pbk)
ISBN: 0-595-65967-5 (cloth)

Printed in the United States of America

To the ghosts of Broadmoor; to those who followed or preceded us; to those we knew and those we did not; and to those who now walk or lie beneath some other fields.

One generation passeth away, and another generation cometh; but the earth abideth forever.

◆   ◆   ◆

All the rivers run into the sea; yet the sea is not full; unto the place from whence the rivers come, thither they return again.

—Words from Ecclesiastes

Contents

Prologue 1
Introduction 3
Chapter 1   Why 5
Chapter 2   The Misty Years 6
Chapter 3   Bogota 9
Chapter 4   Family Relations and Roof Fires 11
Chapter 5   Moving Slow in Bogota 13
Chapter 6   Getting By 17
Chapter 7   Uncle Dirk Was Fun 24
Chapter 8   Uncle Cheat and Aunt Reldie 28
Chapter 9   Bogota Neighbors 31
Chapter 10 Special Memories 37
Chapter 11 School at Bogota 41
Chapter 12 Moving 44
Chapter 13 First Impressions 46
Chapter 14 Broadmoor 51
Chapter 15 The People: Who They Were; How They
            Lived 55
Chapter 16 The Work 62

CHAPTER 17	When Cotton Was King	68
CHAPTER 18	School Days	76
CHAPTER 19	Daddy Was a Beekeeper	84
CHAPTER 20	The Store	87
CHAPTER 21	Membership and Games	90
CHAPTER 22	Other Kids, Other Scenes	94
CHAPTER 23	Mister Sam and Them	98
CHAPTER 24	The Boys	106
CHAPTER 25	More than Skin Deep	110
CHAPTER 26	Floods and Things	112
CHAPTER 27	The Year of Tragedy	116
CHAPTER 28	Getting on With Life	119
CHAPTER 29	Broadmoor, its Character and its Characters	122
CHAPTER 30	Drankin'	127
CHAPTER 31	Waltie	131
CHAPTER 32	A Date That Will Live in Infamy	133
CHAPTER 33	Leaving Broadmoor	138
CHAPTER 34	Mama	139
CHAPTER 35	Vernon	140
CHAPTER 36	Gene	141
CHAPTER 37	Lynn	142
CHAPTER 38	Royce	144
CHAPTER 39	Bueford	153
CHAPTER 40	The Beginning of the End	160
CHAPTER 41	The Tornado	161

Chapter 42	Finality 164
Chapter 43	Other Goodbyes 165
Chapter 44	One Final Fling. 167
Chapter 45	Requiem 169

Acknowledgments

First, we say thank you to our brothers, Lynn and Royce for their free, honest, helpful and well-intentioned advice and criticism when we asked for it.

We are particularly indebted to Sue, who once was a Kennedy but is now an Inlow, who has been helpful in many ways, particularly in her excellent recall of names, relationships, and who married who, and for her research in areas where memory failed us all. We are especially indebted to her for her chilling description of the effects of the deadly tornado as seen through the eyes of a fourteen-year-old.

I, Bueford, want to thank my children who, several years ago, pushed me to write down the material that served as the nucleus of this book.

Now we, both of us, say to our family and our friends; to the teachers who opened our minds; to the mother who showed us we had only to lift up our eyes to find the road that would lead us out of poverty; and to all of those, named and un-named, who provided the memories we use to tell our story, we thank you and hold you warmly in our hearts.

James B (Bueford) Weaver
Union Grove, Alabama

Larry G. (Gene) Weaver
College Park, GA

July, 2003

Prologue

It was a chilly, breezy day in late October but the aging men who stood in that broad, open field did not feel the cold bite of the wind.

They were warmed from within by memories; memories of childhood and early manhood that flooded their minds and echoed in their souls; memories of precious days that, in measured time, were long past but which, in their thoughts, would be never far away. They knew the times they remembered would never be again, but they also knew those days would ever live in the hearts of them who experienced them.

The characters in that scene were us, the surviving sons of James Rufus and Mary Ethel (Reagan) Weaver and on that chill day we were fulfilling a desire held for more than fifty years; a persistent longing that had finally drawn us to come back here; to return once more to this place of our youth.

Once we were five but now one was missing. It had been thirteen years since Vernon had gone to be with Mama and the Lord. Yet, as we that remained stood on this spot that had once so anchored our lives, it was as if his unseen presence made us, for a moment, whole again.

Many years ago the road of life that had brought us here had also led us away in diverse directions but now, finally, some homing instinct had brought us back here together; back to Broadmoor, back to this place of beginnings.

All the old, familiar landmarks that guided us in the past had long since been erased by time but as we stood in that wide, spreading field of several hundred acres our instincts told us our feet were planted on the very spot where the little structure that housed our memories had once stood.

As we surveyed the empty fields, it was difficult to imagine a time when the dwellings of a substantial community could be seen from where we stood for now the single building in view was that of the old church, nearly a mile away.

All trace of those houses was long gone and we felt humbled by the knowledge that, like them, except in our memory, there was no remaining evidence in this place that we had ever existed.

For several moments we were silent. No one spoke. It was as if each of us sensed we were standing on hallowed ground. Then, at once, as if some unseen person or some unheard voice prompted us, we all began to speak as, one by one, memories sprang to life. Except for us, no other living thing was present to hear or see us; no human, no animal, nor even a bird.

Just as a tree that falls in the forest with no one to hear makes no sound, we knew our rushing memories touched no one but us and they existed only in our own minds. And we knew the time was drawing near when, with our passing, the only record of our having come this way would be gone.

But as we claimed that blessed, God-given moment we could imagine He knew and was watching and listening. And perhaps the ghosts of other family and friends, now long gone, but who shared with us those days of yesteryear, were also gathered with us, near but unseen.

We brothers who experienced the moments described here now realize we were, in those days that we seek to recall, too busy living to understand that life is all about making memories.

It may be that this document we now prepare will serve as a memorial and witness to a past that Broadmoor and progress have long since hidden from view. It was here, with eager gusto, we once played out the drama of life. As a family, we loved, we laughed, we bickered, we cried, and we worked and played together. And we dwelt among friends that we now lovingly recall. Our days here we will remember with fondness and no regret and, as we make our preparations soon to move on and make room for those that follow, we leave this record for those who may wish to know that we once passed this way.

May you find our recollections of life on Broadmoor, if not inspiring, at least amusing. And may each of you, wherever life leads you and whatever you do and wherever you dwell, take time to store up along the way warm memories that will one day shield you against the chill October winds of advancing time.

Introduction

First, let us explain about the names.

We were five brothers and each of us was christened by our parents with a first name and a middle name. We are, in order of birth, James Bueford, Vernon Edwin, Larry Gene, Huey Lynn and William Royce. In our youth all but Vernon were commonly called by our middle names. We were then Bueford, Vernon, Gene, Lynn and Royce. Later in life, when we were addressed officially, we were identified by first name and middle initial and, thereafter, we came to be called more commonly by our first names. Thus, Bueford became James or Jim; Gene became Larry; Lynn became Huey and Royce became William or Bill.

In this writing, since we deal mainly with things from our youth, we will use our childhood names.

Now I, Bueford (James B), the oldest of we five brothers, will begin as spokesman for us all.

Much of what you read here was written by me some years ago as I sought, then, to preserve and put down things I feared might fade from memory and be lost. Recently, when my three surviving brothers, Gene, Lynn, Royce, and I, began a more serious effort to assemble our collective memories, I asked Gene, who has some experience as a writer, to take what I had written and edit or re-write it as necessary and, thus, use it as the nucleus of our book. He has faithfully done that and we offer the result to you.

We call this book *Broadmoor*.

Broadmoor is the name of a community where I lived from the time I was eight years old until, at eighteen, I joined the navy. I left Broadmoor then but Broadmoor has never left me. I don't know that I can tell you, or even define in my own mind, what it is that made Broadmoor such an important part of my life; so much a part of me. But listen, if you will, while I tell my story and, in the end, perhaps we both will understand.

In the depths of my mind, Broadmoor has never been just a place. It is an idea, an attitude, a way of life, a period in time. Even now, though the time of Broadmoor is nearly fifty years gone, seldom does a day pass but what some random thought will trigger a memory of my youth and, for a moment, take me back home, back to Broadmoor.

If you are to understand at all, you must first know how it was to be born a poor child, in a poor family in the poor, rural South of the twenties and thirties. So, let me begin there and we will get to Broadmoor in due course.

1
Why

This book is partially the fulfillment of a promise I made to my daughter, Susie, several years ago. Over the years she had heard my brothers and me telling and retelling old stories and was amused by some of them and saddened by others and she suggested that I put some of them down before memory failed me and I promised and I am finally doing so.

What follows are things I have pulled from my memory which may now not be (or may never have been) perfect. We all know that things and events remembered are often seen in a light that differs from reality. Sometimes the light of the present enhances and sometimes it alters our view of the past. There are those of us who tend to recall things past as being either much better or much worse than they were. I guess that would help to explain how a man can tell his children, in all seriousness and believing it is true, how in his childhood he was required to walk four miles to and from school in two feet of snow and it was uphill both ways.

That, of course, is an exaggeration and it is my intent not to exaggerate but to make this, as nearly as possible, a truthful account of one man's journey through a world that was sometimes seen through tears but, more often, with a smile and a happy heart. Perhaps, if the power were mine to do so, there are some things I might change. But, on the other hand, perhaps I wouldn't. The difficult times which, now and then, seemed harsh and unfair were also a tool that helped me build the strength to withstand even more difficult times that were to follow.

On the whole, I can truthfully say mine has been a good life, one blessed by the Lord with family, friends and acquaintances of a value far beyond those I deserved.

2

The Misty Years

The title of this chapter flows from the fact that these are years about which I have no personal memory and I must tell this part of my story in the third person. I am relying, for the stories I tell, on what others, mostly Mama, have since told me.

The first act of this drama begins with what was probably just an ordinary hot July night in the lives of a community of West Tennessee cotton farmers but I would like to think of it as a special night; special for one of us, at least.

The opening scene is set in the home of a poor sharecropper in the community of Bogota. That name was not pronounced like the South American city and was not intended to be. It was properly pronounced "buh-go'-tah" but at that time in that part of the rural south most words ending in an "a" were generally corrupted by changing the "a" sound to "er." Thus, the place of which I speak was locally called "Buh-Goat'-er."

That night, at Bogoter, time had come for a special delivery to the home of James Rufus Weaver, and his young, seventeen year old bride, Mary Ethel, whom he had wooed and won from the family of Robert C. (Corry) and Florence Reagan. What I believe was one of the most reliable reports of that evening's events was later given by Moody Reagan, who is my uncle, Mama's brother. Here is how he told it.

> A woman was going to have a baby so someone had to let the doctor know, so me and a man named Bill Weaver and a boy named Enloe Weaver was to do the job. We started out in a 1922 Model-T Ford to get the doctor. The car had magneto lights on it so if you went too fast you would burn them out. As you can probably guess, that is what happened, somewhere around Bogoter. It was dark and we still had miles to go on a hilly, twisty road and we had to have some kind of light to see by. So we borrowed a kerosene lantern from somebody we knew and took off.
>
> While Bill drove, one of us boys had to set on the front fender and hold the lantern. The light it give was so dim it was just about like a yellow grain of

corn. We were in a mess but we had to go on. There wasn't much traffic on the road, but somewhere out in the hills we almost had a wreck. Somewhere along somebody had left two wagons loaded with stove wood parked on the side of the road. I was the light holder at that time and we were headed straight for the wagons when I caught sight of them. Knowing it would be me, settin' on the front fender, that would be smashed when we hit, I frantically waved and hollered to warn Bill and at the last minute he jerked the wheel and we just did miss the wagons by a hair! But we finally got to Nauvoo where we found a telephone and called the doctor and he agreed to come.

Anyway, we made it so everything worked out all right. The woman had her baby. It was a boy and they named him James Bueford. So all was well and good.

That boy born that night was me; the first of five sons Mama blessed the world with. It was July 26, 1927. The driver on that ride was my Grandpa, William Asbury Weaver. Enloe Weaver, one of the lantern holders, was a cousin, the son of Grandpa's brother, and, of course, Moody was Mama's brother, a couple of years younger than her, then about fifteen.

You can see why I think of that as a special night. But every time I re-read Moody's account of that wild ride through the night I think how much more special it would have been if I could have seen it. What a memory it would have made!

I don't know if angels witness or have anything to do with things like that but, either way, don't you know if they were watching they had a good laugh! Maybe they made, and are saving, a video for me to watch when I get there. Wouldn't that be neat?

We lived there in Tennessee until I was about a year old. Malaria was a health problem where we lived then and I was plagued by it. I think that was the reason we moved to New Mexico, to the town of Roswell. I don't know exactly when we moved there but my brother, Vernon, who was one year and nine months younger than I, was born there on March 28, 1929.

It was while we lived there that I was saved from a possible serious burn by a neighbor friend of Mama's. Mama always said I probably would have burned to death if had not been for the friend. Mama was ironing clothes and using an iron that was heated by gasoline. I never saw one like it that I can remember so I do not know how it worked. Anyway, the iron caught fire and Mama just reacted and threw it out the door. But, when she did that, some of the burning gasoline spilled on me. Mama was so terrified she just stood there screaming. Of course, I was too. The friend, who was there, quickly grabbed me and wrapped me up in her apron and held me until the flames were smothered.

I still wear a small scar on my left cheek as a souvenir of that event. Most folks do not even notice it but I do and, each time I see it, I am reminded that it is just one of the times the Lord has seen fit to spare me. But for His protection, I would not be writing this today.

Sometime in the fall of 1929, Daddy got a letter from his sister, Arelda, that he was desperately needed to help Grandpa Weaver get his cotton crop out. And, like a dutiful son should do, he packed us up and we went back to Tennessee. So ended our sojourn in New Mexico.

Back in Bogota, we moved into the house with Grandpa and Grandma Weaver and Daddy's younger brother, Woodrow. (He was mostly called by nicknames. Some called him Dirk and some Doot; I don't know why.) Mama, Daddy and us two boys had one bedroom we could call our own and we shared the kitchen with Grandpa's family.

Had things been normal, it probably wouldn't have been necessary for us to come back. Grandpa would have found a way to harvest his crop but, as it turned out, it was good we did come back. It was an unusually rainy fall and that kept the harvesters out of the cotton fields and the cotton became worthless. But the worst part, though the two weren't connected, was that was the year the stock market crashed. I believe that was in October and the great depression struck with a vengeance that still sends tremors of dread down the spines of those who experienced it and are still alive today.

Those were terrible times but the hardships they brought, in many cases, heightened the value of the family. For their very survival, families had to cling together. The words, "United we stand; divided we fall" became, not just a motto, but a living truth. No one would want to return to those times but, once they were past, the lesson was there to see. Adversity, even in the extreme, can be a blessing if it teaches the value of family ties. I was too young, in those times, to appreciate this but the time would come when I would see it for myself.

3

Bogota

I said earlier that we lived in a community called Bogota. That's not exactly true. Bogota was our mail address but we lived some four miles from the small gathering of buildings that was Bogota proper. The community then consisted, principally, of two stores, one of which housed the post office; a school for grades one through eight or nine; a cotton gin, and very little else, except for the usual community churches.

At this writing, little of a physical nature has changed in the intervening years except the school is gone. With the coming of school buses and the urbanization of our society, the need for community schools diminished considerably. As the rural population decreased, community schools were eliminated and what children there were were transported to larger, consolidated schools. It was a matter of economics and was necessary, I guess, but it did destroy, or at least diminish, the sense of community.

I realize others might take issue with my saying that and argue that, rather than diminishing, it enlarged the community. That might be true but, in a sense, the closeness that once was was lost forever.

I guess the same argument could be advanced for the world in general. Technological advances in the fields of transportation and communication have transformed us into citizens of a world community and, at the same time, have robbed us of the closeness of the national community we previously enjoyed.

Forgive my straying from my subject into the area of philosophy but the point is that the world is no longer the world I once knew and neither is Bogota.

But to get back to my point: our family didn't actually live in Bogota but on a farm some miles distant. Except for it being on a rural mail route, the farm had no specific address. In those days, rural locations were generally designated by the name of the property owner. Mostly, a holding was not referred to as a farm, but as a "place." Local folk knew who owned what property so when someone spoke of "the Blank place" everybody knew what location that was.

During this period, we, at first, lived on the Butterworth place. Then the property changed hands and, thereafter, though we hadn't moved, our residence was on the Smith place.

4

Family Relations and Roof Fires

Mama and Daddy and me and Vernon, and eventually Gene, continued to live in the house with Grandpa and Grandma and Uncle Dirk for as long as we stayed in that location. Daddy's sister, Aunt Arelda, lived some two hundred yards down the road with her husband, Cheatham Francis Montgomery Tidwell. When I was young it seemed strange to me for anyone to have such a long name. I guess Uncle Cheatham felt the same way for he never used a first name at all. He always did business using only two of his initials and his last name, C. F. Tidwell. We always called him Uncle Cheat and her Aunt 'Reldie.

Living so close to each other then, we may have seemed somewhat like a clan, and I guess we were, but in those days that was not unusual. That was a time of relative immobility and families or other groups who wished to have any kind of continuing relationship had to remain physically close.

The house we lived in had a wood shingle roof and, when they were dry, the shingles could be easily kindled, and regularly were, by sparks flying from the chimney. These events were frightening to me as a small boy but were the source of much amusement when later remembered.

Each time it happened the household followed the same routine, acting out their individual parts as if they were actors in a well-rehearsed play. It was Grandma's role to begin wringing her hands and running about and crying, "Oh Lord! Oh Lord! What are we going to do? What *are* we going to do?" Grandpa, in his starring role, would grab a ladder and a bucket of water and start climbing onto the roof, meanwhile yelling instructions to Daddy to get another bucket and bring him more water. Mama, after making sure we children were all out of the house, would rush about, supporting Grandma in her part and acting as understudy to Daddy's role as water boy.

The others' roles were high drama, but Dirk's (He was then in his early teens.) was more like deadpan comedy and he carried it off like a professional. He would first grab his most valued possession, his guitar, and ensure that it, above all else, was safe. Then he would gather us kids and the guitar and walk a safe distance from the house and would sit down and calmly strum the guitar and watch the action until the fire was extinguished and it was again safe to return.

I think we can rightfully claim that our family invented the Chinese fire drill.

Grandpa always kept ready a supply of new shingles to repair the damage caused by these one-act plays. When the supply began to run low he would simply select a suitable block of oak from the woodpile and, using his sledge and froe, split out a new supply. Grandpa was resourceful that way, and frugal. In those days a careful man didn't just pull out a nail and throw it away as we do today. Grandpa pulled each one, carefully straightened it, and re-used it.

While Grandpa's follow-up role was roof repair man, Grandma's was that of fire marshal. For the next few days, she, being the most experienced and best qualified worrier in the household, would, every few minutes, check the roof for any signs of smoke.

5

Moving Slow in Bogota

Various means of transportation were used in those days, just as is true today, but none of them took us anywhere near mach one.

As one might expect, the most common mode was walking. In those days we didn't walk for our heart and lungs but out of necessity. The person who was limited in his ability to walk was also limited in his range of travel. Walking was a fact and a necessity.

Remembering those times, I am often amused that many of us, now, without embarrassment, will drive to some suitable place so we can walk.

But, in the time I speak of, there were some who adopted strange modes of mobility. There was one boy (I don't remember his name) who was in his late teens or early twenties, who, everywhere he went, rode a steer. I think he did it mostly to be different. I see no other advantage to it. He was probably the kind that, in more modern times, would be driving a vehicle with the body jacked up six feet off the ground.

The boy never said anything, nor did the steer make a sound.

I was then maybe four or five years old and it all seemed really spooky to me. I was afraid of him. If he approached while I was outside playing, I would go up on the porch or inside the house until he passed by. I bet if he were telling this story today he would tell you about the strange kid that always ran for cover when he and his steer came by.

Mule- or horse-drawn wagons probably came in second to walking as the most common mode of travel for short distances. A few people still had buggies but they would have been a luxury in the circles we were a part of. A wagon, however, was the pickup truck of that day. A farmer needed a wagon to haul things in and the same vehicle was used for short family trips.

When I think of any aspect of our life in the era I describe, I often think of Grandpa and thoughts of Grandpa can nearly always produce a laugh.

Grandpa, being the patriarch of our clan, owned the wagon which automatically placed him in charge and the organizer of any excursion in it. To pull the wagon he had a pair of mules. Mules are naturally hard-headed and ornery critters and his were among the orneriest. Mules, once they settle into a job, can be docile and placid but, until they do settle in, some are inclined to run away. "Running away" means they will suddenly, for no apparent reason, bolt and begin to run aimlessly at their top speed and will refuse to obey any effort to stop or re-direct them. Such a runaway will usually last only a few minutes and go for, maybe, a half mile. Once the mules get this out of their system they will again become the docile, obedient beasts they are supposed to be.

It seemed that, at the beginning of any trip, Grandpa's mules insisted on having their runaway. It was their privilege and their right. So any trip with Grandpa, much like the roof fires I have spoken of, could be expected to follow a well-worn script.

While the hitched mules stood quietly, Grandpa would go to a great deal of trouble to load the women and kids and place them just so in the wagon. And when they, and whoever else was going, were properly situated, Grandpa would lightly slap the reins and give the git-up signal and the fun would begin.

The ornery mules, seeing their duty and anxious to do it, would bolt and begin to run away. Meanwhile, Grandpa would be bracing his feet against the front board of the wagon and, with all his might, hauling back on the reins trying in vain to slow the panicked team and shouting, "Whoa! Whoa! You consarned fools, whoa!"

While Grandpa struggled for control and the women and kids screamed in fear of their lives, any other male adults in the wagon, dropped off over the tailgate and, by running at top speed, managed to keep pace with the wagon. One by one, children first, they would pluck those in danger from the wagon and set them down in the road. After saving one, the runner would sprint to catch up with the wagon and repeat this until all those in peril were rescued.

Mostly, at about the time the last rescue was effected, the mules would have had their fun and would slow to a trot and then a walk. Grandpa, then being the only remaining passenger, and now, again in control, he would turn the wagon and begin to retrace his path.

At that time, anyone watching from the point of beginning would see in the distance an empty wagon, pulled by a team of well-behaved mules and, scattered out between, a string of women and kids waiting to be re-loaded one at a time.

When everybody was re-loaded, and only then, would Grandpa again slap the reins and the trip would start all over, quietly this time.

I have never understood why Grandpa, just him and the mules, didn't just go on and have the runaway before he ever loaded his passengers in the first place.

Our mailman, rural carrier Mr. Hascal Reeves, delivered our mail, on horseback when the weather was good, but he had a buggy he used in inclement weather. The buggy had a top and some kind of side curtains he could put up when weather was bad. I don't remember if he used the same horse for both, but he probably did.

There were a few cars around then but not many. Daddy had some kind of vehicle, called a touring car. It had a top of some type of canvas and had snap-on side curtains for when they were needed. I, of course, was too young to know but it was probably the one we went to New Mexico in. I recall later hearing Daddy talk of using a charcoal bucket hung on the dash for heat as the car had no heater. I don't suppose there was any such thing as a car heater in those days. I don't remember ever seeing the car cranked up but it probably was and I was too young to notice.

I do remember the car was the source of the first great disappointment in my life. The one big event in Bogota every year was a fair. I had never attended it but this particular year Daddy promised to take me and Vernon. He would talk to us about it and tell us all the kinds of things we would see there and we became very excited. One of the attractions would be Bogota's own brass band. Daddy told us about one popular band member, called Mexican Bill. He played the tuba. I had no idea what a tuba was but Daddy would illustrate the oompah, oompah sound and our anticipation built even more. We were going to see the fair but also, very importantly, we were going to get to ride there in the car!

Then, only about an hour before time to leave, the bomb dropped. But no lower than our spirits. The car had a flat tire and Daddy was unable to fix it! So we missed the fair and Mexican Bill. To try to imagine how great was my disappointment, just take note of the fact that it is still sharp in my mind to this day.

There were a few airplanes around during those early years but the sight of one was rare. I only remember seeing one or two during the years we lived near Bogota. If a plane was heard overhead everyone dropped whatever they were doing and rushed outside to see it.

I remember a time when I was about five years old and I was sick in bed with the whooping cough and pneumonia. I had been bedfast for about two weeks and, I now understand, my survival had been in doubt. And there came the sound of a plane. It must have been a Sunday for everybody was in the house and they all ran out to see. I remember the last thing Mama said as she was rushing out was, "You stay in that bed. Don't you try to get up!" You know I said, "All right. I will." But the door hadn't closed behind her before I was struggling to get out of bed. I simply couldn't miss the chance to see a real airplane. It could be years before I had another opportunity.

Well, when the others came back in they found me lying unconscious on the floor by the bed. My spirit had been willing but the flesh had been weak.

6

Getting By

Times were hard in those depression years we lived near Bogota but we were more fortunate than some. Those like us who had formed a friendship with Mother Nature and were willing to work hard and use their ingenuity could find a way to survive. And our family was well supplied on all counts. Whatever need developed, Grandpa Weaver could find a way to make do and get by. Our Daddy also apparently inherited the same genes and his veins flowed with the same blood. I never knew either of them to look at a problem and say, "I can't do it." They always said, instead, "I'll find a way."

If a chair wore out and needed a bottom, Grandpa would peel a hickory sapling, split the bark into strips and weave a new one. If he wanted to take the time and make the bottom more permanent, rather than using the bark he would peel off thin strips of the hickory wood and use that for his weave.

If the handle of a hammer or sledge or axe broke, he would split out a block from a selected log and carve a new one.

If he needed a bolt or fitting of some kind for a piece of farm machinery, he would fire up his blacksmith equipment, select a suitable piece of metal from his scrap pile and make one.

Grandpa's scrap pile was a revelation. He didn't sort it or arrange it in any order, but when a piece of metal was needed for any purpose, he would ask himself how long, how wide, how thick, how strong, and he would reach down in his scrap pile and pull out the exact piece required to forge what was needed.

Grandma Weaver (Her name was Cassie Lucille and her maiden name was Craig.) was equally adept at getting things done around the house and, especially, in the kitchen. With her sewing skills she kept Grandpa's overalls and shirts in serviceable condition and would sew for anyone else that asked her. She would mend and patch a garment until it seemed, sometimes, all that was left of the original was the buttons. And when it was, at last, beyond repair, she would save it and use its less-worn parts to patch other items. In that sense, she had a scrap pile of her own.

But my fondest memories of Grandma are in other areas. She never met a baby she didn't like, nor was there a child that didn't like her. She could sit down and "bump" the fussiest baby and lull it into sleep. I said bump for she never used a rocker. She had a straight chair with legs that were worn down short from all the bumping it had seen. She would sit down in it and lean backward until the front legs were clear of the floor and then lean forward, bumping the front legs and lifting the back ones clear. And she would go on, back and forth, back and forth, bump-bump, bump-bump, all the while singing her special, peculiar little song, "Addel ding, addel ding, addel ding di dodie." And she would continue until, shortly, the baby would fall peacefully off to sleep. I never heard anyone else sing Grandma's song. I'm sure she made it up herself.

Grandma wasn't a gourmet cook. She never had anything fancy to cook but she was a good cook. Much of the time she had to cook and bake without sugar because there was no money to buy it and she would substitute sorghum molasses or honey as a sweetener. To the delight of us grandkids, she almost always had a few "tea cakes" hidden around somewhere. She could even cook turnips, not the tastiest vegetable in the garden, that would keep you coming back for more. Somehow she seasoned them with pods of red pepper that gave them a flavor I never found anywhere else.

Her egg custards were also one of my all-time favorites but her Christmas baking was the best of all. She could make a coconut cake that you could hardly wait to taste. She made it with fresh coconuts, using the ground meat as well as the milk. And she used real sugar she had hoarded up for the occasion. She would bake several cakes, including the coconut, at least a week before Christmas and store them in her pie safe. That week seemed like a year to a boy who found a thousand excuses to walk by and look at them, temptation causing his mouth to water every time.

On balance, Grandma as The Provider, was probably at her best in the crises that seemed to come once or twice a year. In those days people had no access to telephones or other ready means of communication. So, if one thought of paying a visit to a friend or relative, he couldn't call up and solicit an invitation. He just loaded up the family and went, never doubting he would be welcomed upon his arrival. It was the custom, then, to take the whole family and plan to stay two or three days. Often the first notice a hostess-to-be had was when some member of the family noted a mule-drawn wagon approaching loaded with uninvited but, nevertheless, welcome guests.

Each time Grandma detected such an unexpected crowd descending upon her, she would freak out and begin wringing her hands and moaning and crying, "Lord, what are we going to do? Us with hardly a bite to eat in the house! Where are they going to sleep? Bill, tell me *what* am I going to do?" But then, as soon as the company got within earshot, her demeanor would undergo a miraculous change and she would run out to meet them and throw her arms around them as if their coming was a pure delight which, as a matter of fact, it was for Grandma loved company. Still, after all the greetings, when Grandma took her station in the kitchen and began rattling pots and pans, you might still hear her mumbling, "Lord, what are they going to eat?"

But that was when Grandma was at her best. Like I said, she was a provider. Why, she could fix potatoes in so many different ways you would have a feast, never realizing there was only one thing on the menu.

For as long as her guests remained, Grandma would be constantly scurrying about. She would have us kids catch up a couple of pullets to fry and a hen to boil with dumplings and would continuously pull from the oven fluffy, brown biscuits and nourishing cornbread and, of course, work her magic with her egg custards for the adults and tea cakes for the children.

At night there would be pallets on the floor for the kids while adults slept several to the bed (properly segregated, of course). Everybody would have a marvelous time and when, at last, the company left, Grandma would wave them out of sight and then, with a sigh, sit down for the first time since they came and begin to rest up for the next occasion when we would hear her start all over again, *"Oh Lord, what are we going to do?"*

The farm we lived on at Bogota was not ours. As I mentioned earlier, it was owned, at first, by Mr. Butterworth and then by a Mr. Smith. As our payment for the privilege of farming it, the owner took a portion of the cotton and corn we produced. At no extra charge we were allowed to use a small plot of ground to grow food and there was a barn and a barn lot for caring for our farm animals; the mules, a cow and a hog or two.

Cash money was so scarce as to be almost non-existent. Practically everything we ate came from the garden and the animals we raised. In season, we picked vegetables fresh from the garden and canned all of the surplus we could. The beans and peas that we didn't eat or can were allowed to dry on the vine and then were picked and stored up for the winter.

We planted and raised substantial crops of both sweet and Irish (pronounced "Arsh") potatoes. Early in the year, when they were not much more than marble size, we would begin to dig the Arsh potatoes, harvesting only enough for one meal at a time. They were very tender and tasty, especially when combined with certain other vegetables. A particularly delicious combination was new potatoes and fresh English peas. Mama or Grandma would cook up a pot of them and add a little flour or something so that the vegetables floated in a light white sauce. When eaten with some hot, crisp, buttered cornbread, like the man says, "It don't git no better'n 'nat!"

In the fall, the sweet potatoes, and the Arsh potatoes that were still in the ground, were harvested and spread in some dry place where they cured out and remained edible for months.

Like all our neighbors, we planted a large plot of turnips which, in the growing season, provided delicious greens for the table, especially when a chunk of fat pork was available for seasoning.

Turnips were an important part of our diet for, if the proper technique, called "hilling up" was used, they could be stored away for use in the cold months of winter. In the late fall, just before the first freeze, the turnips were pulled. A large pile would be laid out on the ground and covered with a thick layer of loose dirt, leaving open a small area on one side of the pile. This area would then be covered with a board or maybe a piece of tin. This cover could later be removed and replaced as access to the hilled-up turnips was required. The covering dirt, which was thick enough to insulate the turnips against freezing, would settle down and become solid enough that rain, when it fell, would mostly drain away. Later, when turnips were needed for the pot, it was a simple matter to remove the cover of the access hole, take out the needed turnips, and replace the cover. Properly constructed and maintained, the turnip hill could provide fresh vegetables all winter long.

Turnips, while they provided a filler for the stomach, were rather bland in taste and required some ingenuity on the part of the cook to make them palatable. While they became, in the depression years, an important staple in the diet of poor country folks, they were not often found on the menu of those who could afford better.

Being so closely identified with the near-famine conditions that then existed, turnips, in the depression, were called by some "Hoover apples" thus, giving due credit to President Herbert Hoover who, many believed, was responsible for the hard times they endured.

Farm people who could afford it, and this included Grandpa and Grandma, kept a cow. One cow produced enough milk and butter for a good-sized family.

Some two or three hogs, slaughtered after frosty weather arrived in the late fall, provided meat through the winter and on through much of the following year.

Many modern-day meat eaters become squeamish at the mere thought of slaughtering the animal whose flesh they consume. In their mind they refuse to associate a big steak or an order of bacon with some cute pig or beautiful white-face steer that, a few days ago, was a living, breathing animal. We, as farm folk, were allowed no such delicacy of thought.

Hog-killing, as we referred to it, would come around about the first decent cold snap of approaching winter. It was a gross, sometimes disgusting, process but all the family, including children, had to involve themselves in it. I see no need, here, to provide distasteful details but you who ever went through it know what I am talking about and, you who have not, just trust me. You don't want to know.

Some years we found ourselves with a hog or two that was not needed for food or for pig production. These were used in barter with others who needed the hogs but had a surplus of something else we could use.

In addition to what was needed to feed our animals, we grew corn to be ground into cornmeal for our own use. There was always someone in the community with a grinding mill and we took our shelled corn to him. Again, no cash was involved. He did the grinding for a share of the meal.

We grew no wheat to be ground into flour. Flour had to be bought and paid for with cash money so, at most of our meals, we ate cornbread.

Every household raised their own chickens and they ran loose in the yard. For the most part they fended for themselves, subsisting on whatever insects or worms they could catch supplemented by scraps of food thrown out the back door by the farm wife. In the spring, those who wished and could afford it, could order baby chicks (advertised as day-old) by mail. The rural carrier would bring them in boxes of twenty-five, fifty or a hundred packed-tight chicks, most of them still alive. After they were unpacked, the chicks required several days of close, tender care. At best, several more would be lost before they could be released to run free in the yard.

Because of the cost involved, and the bother, most people grew their own chicks rather than ordering them by mail. Over a week or so, the farm wife would save her extra eggs until she had a settin' or two. It took a dozen or more eggs to make a settin'. Each spring, in obedience to the mothering instinct, several hens would become "broody," that is, they would begin exhibiting unmistakable signs they were ready to set. The farm wife would prepare a nest for each hen she wanted to set, would fill it with the eggs she had saved and place the broody hen on the eggs. Then, for the next three weeks, the hen very rarely left the nest and, then, for only brief periods. At the end of the three weeks, which must have seemed like years to the hen, she would come down from the nest followed by a new brood of cute little chicks.

In farm communities, settin' hens sometimes provided the basis of social interaction. It was common for the women to swap settin's of eggs. One wife might have mostly Dominican chickens and another White Minorcas or Rhode Island Reds, or some such. One might say, "I been meanin' to get me some of them," and the other would usually respond, "Why, I'll give you a settin,'" to which the first would respond and offer a settin' of hers in exchange. The next thing you knew both would have a yard full of chickens of a different color from what they previously had.

Whatever color the chickens were, they provided eggs, pullets for the frying pan, and more mature chickens for the stew pot. Again, I will spare my more fastidious readers and omit processing details, but the chicken flock was, like the modern freezer, a ready source of food when an unexpected need developed. A chicken that was running free an hour ago was often the entrée in a Sunday dinner for the preacher.

From what I have told you, you can see that country dwellers, for basic subsistence, had little need for cash. They had to buy salt and buy flour if they wanted biscuits, and wanted gravy for sopping with the biscuits. But, except for that, they could eat pretty well on what they grew.

A farmer also grew the food for his animals and, to plant next year's crops, he saved seed from this year. Most men were required, each year, to buy a couple of pairs of overalls and work shirts, a pair of work shoes, some sawmill socks and, probably, at least one pair of long-handle underwear. Every year or so, his wife would petition for a few yards of cloth to make herself a new Sunday dress and she would use the big scraps to make a bonnet and the smaller ones to piece patchwork quilt tops.

But in the worst part of the depression there were no funds available for even these meager purchases. Mama used to talk about the time when Daddy was down to one pair of overalls and had not even the small price of another. When his one pair had to be washed, he would go to bed while she scrubbed them on the rub-board and hung them out to dry in the wind.

I have spoken here in general terms of how farm life was lived in the years of the depression and the following years of recovery. But let me be specific. This was the way *we* lived. We got by.

We survived, but just barely. Through hard work and self-denial and doing without and scrimping and making do, we got by.

For the most part, through the depression years, I was too young to be aware that our family was living hard and, now that I know, I don't weep for us for I realize there were others, in that time, who would have counted our standard of living as luxurious. I can't even imagine the hardship, the deprivation, the humiliation and the deep sorrow that must have been felt by thousands of city mothers and fathers as they struggled to feed their starving families and had no access to a garden plot or a cow or a hog pen or a chicken coop. When I think of them I thank the Lord for letting me be born a country boy.

7

Uncle Dirk Was Fun

Daddy's younger brother, Woodrow, otherwise known as Dirk, was a lot of fun. He was ten or eleven years older than I was but he played a lot with me and Vernon when we were of preschool age. He didn't just do things for us. We had to do things for him too. We had a little push or pedal car that was big enough for the two of us or one of him to ride in. Vernon and I would get in it and Dirk would push us around the house. Then we would have to get out and push *him* around in it. Twice. I guess that was fair.

He had a toy fire truck, the finest I ever saw, or at least I thought so at the time. It was constructed of sturdy metal and could be steered by its little steering wheel. It had a tank that would hold water and it had a hose on it and the ladders that could be removed and extended. It was probably about eighteen inches long. It was a dandy for that time and was just like new for he only got it out and played with it at Christmas time. He would let Vernon and me play with it but only for a little while and then under his close supervision.

I don't know when he got his truck but I do know it was still like new when, years later, sometime in the forties, Dirk's own son, Everett, was playing with it and broke it.

Grandpa used to get kind of aggravated at Dirk because he never took anything serious. He was just full of foolishness.

We lived in a time that chicken stealing was a common occurrence. One might wonder, now, why on earth someone would want to steal a chicken. I'll explain. As I have said, cash money, or the opportunity to earn some, was almost nonexistent. And there were lots of ordinarily honest people who had been brought down to the point they would steal, if they had to, to feed their hungry children.

And there was a market for chickens. There were businesses in the nearby town of Dyersburg where one could walk in with live chickens and sell them for a few cents each. Many were legitimately sold that way every day. If one had more chickens than he needed, he would catch up a few of them, tie their feet together in bunches of four or five, toss the now helpless birds into his wagon or the trunk of his car, and take them to market. The buyer, of course, had no way of knowing if the seller was the legitimate owner.

So, chicken-stealing did occur. And Grandma was constantly concerned that she was going to be a victim. Let there be the slightest clucking or other noise emanating from the henhouse at night and Grandma was ready to rush out and personally take the suspected thieves into custody. She would begin poking Grandpa and saying, "Get up, Bill, get up! Somebody's in the chickens!" Grandpa, of course, would try to shush her and go back to sleep, but Grandma wasn't having any. She would keep poking and nagging and urging him until he crawled out of bed. He would light the lantern that hung by the back door, hand it to Grandma and get his shotgun. Then, he in his underwear and Grandma in her gown; her continually fussing so that any actual thief would surely have been alerted and be long gone, they would sally forth to protect their property.

Well, knowing all this, Dirk and some of his cousins or friends couldn't resist, from time to time, having a little fun. If they came in after dark, after the chickens, and Grandma and Grandpa, had gone to bed, they would take a stick of some kind and start jabbing at the hens on the roost. The chickens, of course, would react to these indignities and begin to cluck and fuss. The boys would continue the game until they heard Grandma and Grandpa coming with lantern and gun and a great deal of bickering and then they would run down through the cornfield or cotton patch and, when they reached a place of safety, would collapse in laughter.

The boys weren't worried that they would suffer any harm for they knew Grandpa never kept his shotgun loaded.

Then one night they were having their fun when Grandpa changed the rules of the game. I don't remember if he deliberately loaded the gun or, maybe, he had been out hunting and neglected to unload it, but, that night, he came out with a charged weapon. Then, as he neared the henhouse, there, in the dim light near the door, stood a figure. Finally, he thought, here was a real chicken thief!

Reacting, I guess, to fear and shock, and forgetting for the moment that he would never shoot at another human being in any circumstance, Grandpa threw his gun to shoulder and blasted away. Only then, as the figure collapsed and fluttered to the ground, did he recall that, the previous afternoon, Grandma had washed his other pair of longhandle underwear and left them hanging on the clothesline! Needless to say, because of Grandpa's marksmanship, the long johns were never the same. Of course, before the gunfire, Dirk and his cronies had long gone and it wasn't a close call, but I think, after that, there were fewer disturbances around the henhouse at night.

Dirk could not only be funny ha-ha, he was sometimes funny peculiar. When he was going to high school at Bogota he had to travel on foot the four or five miles to school. He would run a good portion of that distance and he had heard somewhere, and believed, that drinking a glass of milk with raw eggs in it would give you longer wind. So, every day, as soon as he got home from school, he would mix up his milk and eggs and drink it down. I don't know if it helped or not but he declared it did.

In those days some people complained of a condition, mostly self-diagnosed, known as catarrh (pronounced ka-tar'). This was an inflammation of the mucus membrane of the nose and throat and it caused a little sniffle and maybe a little throat congestion. Anyway, the accepted treatment was spraying the area with a salt water solution. Dirk, whether it was true or not, imagined he had catarrh and would spray a couple of times a day. He would make a big production of it, spraying and snorting and blowing and generally making strange noises. He did that for years. I guess he finally cured himself for, years later, after he came back from service in the army, I noticed he didn't spray any more.

Having mentioned Dirk and the army, I will go ahead and tell you a little anecdote he told us about that. He was finally drafted in the latter part of World War II and, with the war in Europe winding down, found himself a tank driver somewhere in Germany. Moving slowly through some small town, he rounded a corner and came face to face with a German Tiger tank. That was apparently as big a surprise to the German crew as it was to the Americans for both stopped in their tracks, sat looking at each other for a moment at point-blank range and, without firing a shot, both slowly backed around a corner and retreated. When, a little later, Dirk and his crew, out of embarrassment, I guess, eased back around the corner, the German was gone. Dirk said they didn't try too hard to find him.

I will tell one more story about Dirk. Sometimes, in cotton-chopping season, Grandpa would hire a few extra hands and assign Dirk, after he got older, as a sort of field leader, it being his job to keep everybody moving so that Grandpa would get his money's worth. Dirk turned out not to be a hard supervisor but he was an entertaining one. He knew a million jokes clean enough to tell in mixed company and he told them all. He could tell jokes all day long and never repeat himself.

Grandpa didn't do much cotton-chopping but, sometimes, when he wasn't sure we were working hard enough, he would come out to the field and take a hoe and start whanging away, exhorting us to "Come on; come on!" These spurts wouldn't last long before Grandpa, having made his point, would take his hoe and go off to find some easier work. As soon as Grandpa left, Dirk would tell us, "Don't pay any attention to Pa. He will work you to death if you let him!" Then he would start in again, "Did I tell you the one about…?"

Cotton chopping was never fun, but it was a lot easier when Dirk was the field leader.

8

Uncle Cheat and Aunt Reldie

Uncle Cheat and Aunt Arelda (We called her Aunt Reldie), were good folk but they were a little different. They couldn't have children and they, especially her, didn't want kids around too much. I don't say that to be mean. It was just a fact and it alerts you to the truth that life with them was a little different.

I want to limit this chapter to three events that occurred while we lived in the Bogota community.

Vernon and I spent the night of March 24, 1931, at Aunt Reldie's and we were pretty excited about that. I don't remember what we did there but I'm sure it wasn't much because we would have had to be on our best behavior but I do well remember the next morning. We were taken back home pretty early because there was something there they wanted us to see.

It was our new brother, Gene, who had been born the previous night. We didn't even know the baby was coming. These days even very young children are allowed to see and feel and listen to Mommy's big belly and watch it move but, in those days, two year old kids (like Vernon) and those going-on-four (like me) didn't notice things like that. We had never seen a new baby up close before but we both spotted something that didn't seem right. We didn't say anything right way, and didn't know if we should say anything at all, but we noticed there were big, dark brown, almost black, splotches all over the baby's face. Finally, we had to say something, and when we did, the adults laughed and assured us there was nothing wrong with him. It was some kind of medicine they put in a newborn's eyes then, I guess to prevent infection.

The blotches disappeared in a few days and the baby turned out to be a brother we have always been proud of, even though we did have some doubts about him in the beginning.

There was another time, I don't remember when or why, Vernon and I had been permitted to go to Aunt Reldie's and we were playing under the house. In that time, none of the farm houses were underpinned but were set up on blocks high enough that kids could easily get up under them and play. And that was fun; kind of like having a big play-house. It was cool and the dirt under the house would get loose and easily formed or moved about. The chickens also liked to get under there and fluff their feathers in the dust and that helped keep the dirt loose.

We children liked to shape the loose dirt and build it into roads and such. An empty snuff bottle was just the right size and shape to become, in our imagination, a car or a truck to push along our roads.

On this occasion that I remember, while playing under Aunt Reldie's house, one of us found a penny. Now, we had never owned a penny before. We had no idea what we could buy with it but we were sure it would be a lot. I don't remember which of us got to carry the penny but I do remember how anxious and thrilled we were to show our fortune to Mama.

But, when we did, she burst our bubble and, at the same time, taught us a lesson I never forgot. She asked us, sternly, "Where did you get that?" and we told her. And, as you can probably guess, Mama told us, "That's not yours. You go back over there right now and you give that penny to your Aunt Reldie and tell her where you got it. And you apologize for taking it!"

Of course we did exactly as Mama instructed us to do. We went back to Aunt Reldie and held the penny out to her *and she took it and kept it!*

To this day, I don't know what Aunt Reldie was thinking in taking the treasure we had found. She had no need for it. But I know Mama's intent was to teach a lesson. She knew we weren't thieves but she also knew there is a difference between honesty and the absence of thievery. That was a lesson I have never forgotten.

Aunt Reldie was a faithful subscriber to a weekly newspaper that was published in Dyersburg under the name of *The State Gazette*. She was a subscriber for as long as I remember, I think up to the day she died. She was very careful of her paper and would keep each copy for long periods of time. I learned to read from the comic section of that paper. She didn't like for me to touch it for she thought I would tear it. But I got to see enough of it while she or someone else was holding it that I learned to read pretty good.

Aunt Reldie didn't believe I could read but one day she agreed to let me try and I proved to her I could. After that she would let me look at the paper while she was near enough to keep an eye on me.

I could read pretty well when I was six years old even though I had never attended school yet. Beginning with my interest in Aunt Reldie's newspaper, I acquired an interest in reading that has been an important educational tool throughout my life and it has rewarded me with untold hours of pleasure.

9

Bogota Neighbors

I was too young to know all our neighbors at Bogota but I will tell you of a few of them. The first two I will mention stand out in memory because they were different from the rest of us in some way. They, like all the others I have mentioned, or will mention, were real people who, like the rest of us, looked adversity in the face and, with courage and determination, defeated it. But, because of their individual peculiarities, they were sometimes looked down on by their neighbors. Let me tell about them and let you judge whether such a view was justified.

Mr. W, and his wife and daughter, lived near us. There is one particular thing about him that stands out in my memory. An important piece of a dirt farmer's equipment was his turning plow. Each year, the plow was used in one of the early steps in preparing the land to receive the seeds of the new crop. Pulled by a team of mules, and guided by the farmer, the plow was used to loosen and turn over the soil. As the work progressed from field to field, the plow, of course, had to be moved. Every farmer I ever knew, except Mr. W, would lay the plow over on its side so that the blade wasn't digging in, and would let the mules drag it to the new location. Mr. W didn't do that. He would unhitch the team from the plow, lift the heavy plow to this shoulder, and *carry* it to the new location.

All the neighbors thought this was foolish but Mr. W said it saved wear and tear and the dulling of the blade of the plow. He was probably right, up to a point, but that was a lot of effort for a small return.

Mr. W had a long, white beard like Santa Claus and he never shaved it off. That seemed strange to me and I was afraid of him. He was never mean or threatening to me in any way but I would never go near his house. Though there was no reason for it, I was afraid something very scary was going on there, maybe something to do with witches.

The W family was kind of withdrawn from the community and the community was withdrawn from them. I didn't know then, and I wonder now, if there was a reason. As a little boy I hadn't yet learned that we, as a society, tend to treat those who are different from us in an unkind manner. I wonder, now, if it would have made a difference if the rest of the community had offered the W family a friendly arm around the shoulder and a kind word of encouragement rather than the Pharisaic stonewall treatment.

Then there was a Mrs. H who lived down the road from us in the opposite direction from Mr. W. While Vernon and I were afraid there might be witches at the W House, we had no doubt about Mrs. H. We were convinced she *was* a witch. I think, now, the idea probably originated with some joking reference by one of the adults but it was no joke to us. To reach Aunt Reldie's house or that of some children we liked to play with, we had to go by Mrs. H's house and that required a great deal of courage on our part.

Mrs. H seemed to have a store of unusual knowledge and that may have been a part of mine and Vernon's fear of her. Once, Vernon developed some kind of sore behind his ear that was not responding to Mama's home remedies. It only got worse. Although country people of that era seldom sought the help of a doctor, Mama and Daddy became so concerned that they took Vernon to the doctor on two occasions. But the doctor couldn't cure him either.

Then Mrs. H took the case. She told Mama to get a piece of a certain kind of yarn thread, something like knitting thread, and to heat it on the stove until it became a powder. She said put the powder on the sore and it would heal within a week.

Mama, at first, passed this advice off as some sort of foolishness but, after they saw the doctor and the sore only got worse, she decided it could do no harm to try it. She tried it and it worked. The sore healed right up. It might have been that something else killed the infection, but maybe Mrs. H. did have special powers.

Mrs. H visited in our house on a number of occasions and never posed any overt threat to us. But that didn't matter to me and Vernon. We were still scared of her. I wonder if she ever knew.

There was another person who lived down the road from us, I will call her Miss Dee, who followed, for our community at least, an unusual line of work. Where she got her training or motivation, I never learned, and, as a kid, I had no real understanding of what, exactly, her job was, except she provided some sort of social service of which the other ladies of the community disapproved.

As I grew older, and a little wiser, I learned that Miss Dee had, at an early age, become aware that nature had endowed her with certain, er, attributes for which there was an ongoing demand. Recognizing this, she devised a marketing program that freed her from the more strenuous work and longer hours involved in picking cotton. And, she wouldn't have to be on her feet all day and she could do her work at home.

There were some who did not whole heartedly approve of her choice of profession but, while they didn't embrace her (well, I mean as a community) neither did they shun or chastise her for it as she moved among them. Miss Dee seemed to be happy in her work which she plied throughout a long career that extended from youth to beyond normal retirement age, managing along the way to feed and clothe the several children she bore.

While I (and I swear it's true) was never a customer, I know for a fact that, in some families, three generations, that is grandfather, father and son, benefited from her skillfully applied and therapeutic services.

Now, I don't believe this, but my own dear grandpa was regularly accused by Grandma of sneaking off for business meetings with Miss Dee. He denied there was any truth to her accusations but there came a day when she believed she proved her case.

There was this one particular field he worked that had a small wood growing at one end of it and this was where Grandma suspected Grandpa was cultivating something more than cotton. The location was some distance from the house but Grandma, using the old army field glasses that Uncle Will Craig had brought back from the war, could see him plainly if he stayed in the field. But, ah-ha! Now and then she would see him stop his team and go into the woods and stay longer than she thought he ought. Maybe he was just answering a call of nature or catching a little rest in the shade of the trees but Grandma was convinced there was another, less innocent, explanation and, when Grandpa would come to the house, she would light in on him and he would, or course, deny any wrongdoing.

Well, I have mentioned before that Dirk was a prankster, him and some of his ornery cousins and friends, and, of course, they knew of Grandma's suspicions and her field glasses. One day, when Grandpa was working in the far field, they borrowed some female garments and a bonnet from the clothesline and concealed themselves in the woods. Then, every time Grandpa would plow out to the end of a row by the woods, one of them, in dress and bonnet, would run out and throw their arms around Grandpa and pretend they were trying to drag him into the bushes. All the while Grandma had him under surveillance. Grandpa would try to fight them off but, from her vantage point, Grandma just saw this as more slap-and-tickle. Before the pranksters were through with Grandpa that day, it would have been hard to say which was more steamed, Grandma or her glasses.

She had known it all along and now she had him. She had finally caught the no-good scoundrel doing what she had been accusing him of for years! This time she had seen it with her own eyes!

Grandpa never convinced her it was just a prank and neither the boys nor Miss Dee were talking.

Down the road a little way past Mrs. H there lived the Nichols family. The parents were Harry and Pauline and they had three children: Doris, who was about my age; Rice A., near Vernon's age; and Edward, about the same age as Gene. In a manner that I thought unusual, everybody always called the older boy by his first name and initial, Rice A. But they pronounced it so it sounded like they were saying "Ri-say." As I recall, Ri-say was named for a relative, perhaps an uncle, who was a local person of some influence.

There were other children in the community but they lived farther away so we didn't become as close to them as we did the Nichols kids, with whom we became best friends. Even after we moved away, our families remained close and my brothers and I would occasionally come back and spend the night at the Nichols house.

The Nichols's owned their own farm and enjoyed an affluence far beyond ours but that didn't seem to matter to them. I recall that Miss Pauline had a gasoline powered automatic washing machine, a Maytag, and, as far as I can recall, it was the only one in the community at the time.

On their property, out behind their barn, which was behind the house, the Nichols's had a pond. The pond served as a watering place for the livestock and a place for their few ducks and geese to do whatever it is ducks and geese do. There was another creature that lived in the pond, a very large logger-head snapping turtle. He was seldom seen but he apparently considered it his pond. There was reason to believe that he might have been responsible for an occasional reduction in the inventory of ducks and geese.

From childhood on, we maintained our friendship with the Nichols family.

Sadly, Ri-say was killed in action during the Korean conflict. He was an infantry squad leader and one of his cousins was a member of the squad and was later able to report on the action. As the cousin told the story, the squad was on a Korean mountain side and a large force of Chinese soldiers was advancing and about to over run their position. To save the lives of his men, and with full and certain knowledge of the consequences of his actions, Ri-say ordered them to evacuate, telling them he would stay and draw the enemy fire and cover their retreat as long as he could. The others took the only chance they had and escaped but Ri-say, true to his promise, stayed behind. When they last saw him, he was standing alone, in plain view of the enemy, firing an automatic rifle into the onrushing horde.

It was a long time later, after the cease-fire, that his body came home. Ri-say was buried with full military honors but, of course, the casket was closed. It was said that his mother, Miss Pauline, expressed some concern that the remains in the casket were, in fact, those of her son. However, she was philosophical about it and said, whoever the boy was, she would give him a proper burial and hope that, somewhere, some other mother would do the same for Ri-say.

On behalf of his fallen son, Rice A's father accepted his Silver Star.

We, his proud friends, believe that, by his actions in deliberately and knowingly sacrificing his own life to save those of his friends, Rice A. earned, and should have been awarded, the Congressional Medal.

The Nichols's were extremely honorable people. But that could not be said about all the people of Bogota. There was man, I will call him Mr. J, who lived not far from us. If Bogota had had a mafia, Mr. J would have been the godfather. I was too young, then, to give you a first-person account of Mr. J's activities, but I believe the stories that widely circulated were true. Anyway, I will tell them to you as I heard them told.

The making of moonshine whiskey was a thriving business around Bogota and Mr. J owned the operation but he hired others to do the work and take the risks. When the law found and raided one of his stills only the operators, not Mr. J, took the fall. Their sentence was always a year and a day. It was said Mr. J paid his employees for their inconvenience and saw their families were fed while they were away.

Mr. J. drove a fancy car. There was a story (and I won't vouch for this one.) that he took out an insurance policy on one of his employees. He then ordered the man to lie down in the road so that Mr. J could back over him with the car and cause enough injury that he could make a claim against the insurance. It was a good plan but there was a hitch. He could get the man to lie down in position but, each time Mr. J began to back up, the man would lose his nerve and jump and run. As the story continues, Mr. J finally lost his temper and the man suffered considerable injuries but not the kind that would support a claim against the insurance company.

There is another story, one that did not involve Mr. J, but one of which I had personal knowledge. I don't recall any names but the principals in the affair were two men and a woman. (Sound familiar?) One of the men, a very jealous sort, was dating the woman when the other began to move in and, also, to date her. One day the second man, coming home from the fields, was riding his mule past the house of the first man when someone shot and killed him.

Guess who was the prime suspect. After what must have been a brilliant investigation, the first suitor wound up going to prison for a whole year, which seems mighty little punishment for such a crime.

It is time to leave this part of my narrative but let us not do so on the grim note of the preceding story. I'll tell you another.

From time to time in our community, as I guess would be true of most, some crime would be committed and the perpetrator would be on the loose. Such a circumstance would provide the local men, usually including Uncle Cheat, with all the excuse they required to launch a manhunt. I don't think it mattered whether the hunted man had been seen in the neighborhood or which direction he was thought to be headed. The word would go out and a quickly formed posse, armed to the hilt, would gather and take up their position at The Black Bridge, so named because of the color of the creosote used to preserve its timbers. The bridge was on the main road, which was the most obvious escape route for anyone fleeing Bogota justice. There, in a shady, comfortable place under the bridge, the hunters would lie in wait for the fleeing felon, meanwhile telling lies and nipping on whatever anyone had brought along to be nipped on. And woe be unto any fugitive foolish enough to try to break through their dragnet!

10

Special Memories

On the night of November 19–20, 1934, Vernon and I, and Gene this time, once again spent the night away from home. Yep. You guessed it. Mama was giving us another brother. She named him Huey Lynn but Uncle Cheat immediately assigned him a nickname, "Kingfish." That nickname came from Huey P. Long, the well-known Louisiana politician of that day, who was also known as The Kingfish. To further confuse the issue (and Lynn) Aunt 'Reldie insisted on calling him Huey P., still with Mr. Long in mind. She called him that, I guess, for as long as she lived.

We don't know how old Lynn was before he knew his real name.

This next glimpse I offer may seem to you a little gross so you might want to skip it but, if you want to hang with me, you may gain a little more insight into country life as it was lived in those days.

Every household, then, kept a large container in the kitchen into which was deposited scraps of food and waste water; things that, for animals, would be edible. The container was called the slop bucket. In that time, there were no kitchen garbage dispose-alls or garbage men to come by and pick up the trash. People had a different kind of disposal service. It was call The Hogs.

Hogs would eat anything, and with great relish, and it would have been considered wasteful to throw away anything humans didn't want to eat but the hogs would. Farm folk kept a trough in the hog pen and, about once a day, they would carry the slop out and dump it in the trough. The hogs would come running and squealing and climbing over each other and would dive in and, with a great amount of loud sucking and gobbling and munching, would devour it in no time flat. One had to wonder how anything could possibly be as delicious as the slop seemed to be to the hogs.

There was a common country saying in that time, used to explain a person's special longing for, or attraction to, something. People would say, "Why, he loves that like a hog loves slop!" Only if you had ever seen a bunch of hogs fighting to get to the trough would you fully understand what that meant.

But to get on with my story: Vernon, when he was just old enough to crawl and toddle around, discovered the slop bucket. And he must have either thought he was a pig or that the goodies in the bucket were too good to be left for the pigs and, if he could catch the grown-ups not looking, he would sneak into the kitchen and retrieve a juicy biscuit for his own consumption. To prevent this, he had to be watched all the time but Vernon was too sly and would sometimes sneak away and you would hear someone yell, "Vernon, what have you got? Lord, that young'un has been in the slop bucket again! What are we going to do with him?" And the struggle to wrest Vernon's treat away would begin. But it was a battle for he didn't give up his biscuits too easily.

Later, when we children got older and it was plain Vernon was developing a more sturdy and well-built body than the rest of us, the adults must have begun to have second thoughts. Perhaps they should not only have left Vernon alone but should have encouraged the rest of us to develop similar tastes.

Vernon was not only somewhat of a pig over his food, he was more nervy and adventurous than most children. I don't remember all the details, but there was a time when the adults had found a grounded owl that had apparently become confused and they brought him into the house for all to see. The owl, while obviously scared, was subdued and quiet and they set him on the headboard of a bed where we could all see him.

The owl looked dangerous to me and I was scared of him and hung back but Vernon, then about two, kept edging closer and closer. Finally, my concern got the better of me and I cried out to Vernon, "Come back, he might hurt you." And Vernon replied, "Hunh-unh, Bubba; I'll kill him with the poker!" Everyone but me thought that was hilarious and it became one of the family stories that, over the years, was told and laughed about over and over.

It wasn't funny to me for I was still scared. Anyway, after a while, the owl was released and we all survived and, eventually, even I began to see the humor in it.

It was not unusual for Grandpa or Daddy or Uncle Cheat to capture some small animal or a bird and cage it for a brief time so it could be observed up close.

One time there was this crow. I don't know how they caught it but they kept it in a cage in the house for a while. Also in the house, in the kitchen, we, as was the custom of farm families then, kept a fifty-pound container (called a "stand") of lard. That is what we used as cooking fat. This may cause some of you to cringe, now, for there is no telling how much cholesterol is contained in fifty pounds of hog fat, but, in those days, nobody had ever heard of cholesterol.

Anyway, one day, while the crow was in residence, the whole family was absent for a time and when we came back we were met with a sorry sight. Somehow, while we were gone, that crow (Crows are very clever.) had managed to get out of his cage and had found some way to pry the lid off the stand of lard and get into it. What we found upon our return was a very messy kitchen and one well-greased crow! He was a pitiful sight.

What were we to do? As a first consideration, could we salvage what remained of the lard or should we dispose of it all? Being frugal farm folk, we couldn't bring ourselves to just throw away anything so valuable. We decided to skim off the obviously contaminated part and preserve the rest.

The crow? Well, we should have just wrung his neck and fed his carcass to the hogs but were too soft-hearted to do so. We rubbed him down as best we could, gave him time for his feathers to fluff out, and turned him loose.

I have heard that some crows can, like a parrot, learn to talk. Can you picture this guy, later on, strutting about and making up some story to explain to all the admiring lady crows how he got all them glossy feathers?

People did a lot of things in those days to make a living. Honest John was a sort of a traveling salesman of the times but we called him a peddler. He didn't just come by and take orders and, when he returned to the warehouse, have your order shipped by UPS or Fed-Ex. He carried his entire stock in a pack on his back. He sold needles and pins and thread and small bottles of vanilla flavoring and some patent medicines and the like. He walked everywhere he went and must have covered a large territory for he only came by our house once a year.

Honest John was further dissimilar to today's traveling merchandiser in that he didn't stop off each night in the local Holiday Inn. Somehow, he arranged his schedule so that he would arrive at our house late in the afternoon. Our house, like many in that time, was built in two sections that were connected by a large covered area. Today, the open area would be called a breezeway but then was commonly called a dog-trot.

That's where Honest John would sleep; out of the rain if it came, but otherwise exposed to whatever mother nature had to offer. He was always given an invitation to come inside but he always declined.

I didn't give it any thought then but I have since wondered how he could work out his schedule so that he always arrived at our house at the proper time to make his sale and spend the night. We fed him supper, and breakfast the next morning, and he would go on his way with a promise to see us next year.

There came a year when we said goodbye; see you next year, and he said "No, you will never see Honest John again." And we didn't. He didn't explain and we didn't know what plan or premonition he had but it was kind of sad and I have often wondered why; what happened to Honest John?

11

School at Bogota

I added a new dimension to my life in my seventh year. I started to school. At Bogota. I didn't start at the customary age of six for Daddy and Mama thought I was too young for the four-mile walk there and the same distance home. But when I did start, I walked every day, except for the first day when Daddy took me.

I think I shall never forget that first day. I was so excited at getting to go. Daddy took me in the wagon. He tied the mules to something at the store that was close to the school and we walked over. We found my room where several children who had already arrived had gathered. I didn't know any of them. Others continued to come in. I was getting a little nervous for I didn't know what to do and then the teacher, Miss Fisher, came in and told us her name. I guess she recognized my look of bewilderment and she told me we would wait a few minutes until everybody was there and she would show me what to do. She showed me where to sit and said that would be my very own seat at school.

I began to relax and was feeling better when I noticed Daddy wasn't there anymore. He had told me he would be back for me but, at the moment, I didn't know where he was and I began to worry how I was going to find my way home, if he didn't come for me.

That first day we only stayed long enough to get enrolled and a few other things and, when that was done, sure 'nuff, Daddy came to get me and I was one relieved and happy boy when I saw him.

The second day went better. Daddy didn't go with me but I didn't exactly go alone. There were two or three other kids that lived near me. I started out with them and we picked up a few more in the group as we went along.

I don't remember what I learned that first day of class, except for one thing. I learned that, when becoming associated with a new group or a new activity, one of the first things you must learn is their language or manner of expression. I not only found that to be true that first day of school but have also found it true all along my journey through life.

One of the first things Miss Fisher asked the class was whether any of us knew our numbers and letters. When nobody raised their hand, she said, "I want you to begin by learning these." and she wrote some numbers, I think it was one through ten, on the blackboard, along with some letters of the alphabet.

When I saw what she meant, I spoke up and said, "Oh, you mean the 1-2-3's and the a-b-c's." And I told her I could say the 1-2-3's to a hundred and I knew all my a-b-c's. I don't think she believed me at first but when she asked me to say them I did.

That might not seem such a big deal but it sure was a confidence builder for me at the time. I realized, then, that I might be a poor country boy but that didn't mean I couldn't compete in the larger world. It may be that has been as much help to me along the way as any lesson I ever learned.

Miss Fisher had her ways of maintaining discipline in the classroom. Most of the time that wasn't a problem but if one of us got too stubborn or rambunctious she used a ruler to paddle the palm of his hand. The ruler could sting, but the most punishing thing she did to an unruly boy was make him sit in the same seat with a girl! What humiliation! The seats were narrow so that you had to sit close and maybe even actually *touch* the girl. One good thing; the other boys couldn't laugh at you or Miss Fisher would, in a minute, have them up and suffering the same punishment.

At that time, the school provided no lunch or lunchroom. Students brought their lunch from home. Usually, several of the boys in my class would gather in a special spot on the porch or in the schoolyard while we ate. Mama, when she packed my lunch, would, if she could, include something sweet, such as a tea cake or a fried pie.

One boy, who was bigger than the rest of us, used to come around our group, hoping to get some of our lunch. I would give him a bite of my sweet stuff but he began to just grab the whole thing and run off with it. That happened a few times and he got away with it but I made up my mind to try to do something about that and, the next time, I was laying for him.

He walked up to the edge of the porch where we were sitting and grabbed my food but he didn't get away with it. In a second, I was off that porch and right on top of him and, since I had the advantage of height and surprise and momentum, he went down. Shocked, I guess, at my audacity in attacking him, he began trying to give my food back to me, all the while pretending it was just a joke; that he didn't really intend to take it. In full capitulation, and with a look in his eyes I couldn't decipher, he was actually begging me to take it back and, after that, he never took anybody's food again.

It's strange how one will remember something like that all his life. At the time I looked upon this boy as just a boorish, overbearing tough to whom I had taught a lesson and I was sure I did the right thing. But later I began to wonder if there was another explanation. The boy was bigger and stronger than me and could have easily overcome my initial assault and could have enforced his will. But he didn't and I have thought about that.

I don't remember that I ever saw that boy with a lunch of his own. Maybe he didn't have one. I hope that wasn't true but I will never know. And I don't think I want to know, for it would break my heart even now if I knew the boy had to go hungry all day and I didn't share my lunch with him.

12

Moving

It was 1935 when we moved from our familiar surroundings at Bogota to the Broadmoor community. I don't remember the exact time but I am sure it would have been soon after the first of the year and before time to start farming operations in the spring. That would have been the customary time for a farm family to move.

I do remember that, at first, I didn't much like the idea of moving. I didn't want to leave our friends, the Nichols children, but the adults promised I would be able to come back and see them once in a while. So, with the thrilling prospect of seeing what lay beyond the far horizon, and with the comforting assurance I would be able to come back and visit old, familiar places, I began to get excited.

As it turned out, the horizon was not all that far. The distance we moved was no more than three miles if we took all the shortcuts but moving was still a world class adventure to a seven-going-on-eight-year-old boy.

We moved in a wagon, the previously described pick-up truck of the day. All three families moved; Grandpa and Grandma and Dirk; Mama and Daddy and us kids, four of us at that time; and Aunt Reldie and Cheat. None of us had a lot of furniture to move but it still took several trips and, I think, two days, to move our household goods and the animals and the farming equipment. As I remember, the women folk went over in one of the early trips and began getting the new houses organized and set up while the men moved the rest of the stuff. I think we children, too young to be of any help to the men, accompanied the women. Our job, self-assigned, of course, was to scout and explore and learn the layout of this new land.

In that day and time, many roads thought of as improved were not much more than dirt lanes. In the main, their improvement amounted to running a road grader over them a couple of times a year to smooth out the worst bumps. We could have used those roads in our move but the trip would have been at least twice as long. Instead, we took a more direct route using field roads. These were trails laid out and used by farmers to travel from field to field and from farm to farm. If one was familiar with the country, he could use them to move cross-country in a more or less straight line.

Field roads, however, sometimes presented a problem, especially in the wetter seasons. They were muddy and soft and one might encounter places where the wheels of a loaded wagon would sink deep into the wet soil.

On the trip I was on during the move, we found ourselves in such a spot. The wagon wheels sank in almost up to the hubs and the mules couldn't move it. We had to hitch up a second team to get more power. Then, with a great deal of hollering and urging and rein-slapping by the driver and snorting and hunkering down and see-sawing on the part of the four-mule team, the wagon finally came free. This added one more thrill to a young boy's adventure but it didn't appear that the adults looked at it in the same light. Next time, they made a wide detour around that mud hole.

Finally, after two hard days of moving, and several more of getting things properly placed and stored at the new place, we began to settle in as residents of Broadmoor.

13

First Impressions

This place was better than the one we had left. One advantage I recognized right away. For as far back as I could remember, Me and Mama and Daddy and the other kids had lived in the house with Grandma and Grandpa. Here, we had an entire house of our very own and it was a large house, having two whole rooms!

Later on, I realized there might have been better pickings. We and the rest of the clan occupied a cluster of three houses and our family got the smallest of the lot. Grandpa's family and Cheat and Aunt Reldie each had a house with four full rooms and each had a nice, big front porch and, of course, a back porch. Their places also had outbuildings. Grandpa had a smoke-house with an attached, covered shed which he used as a work area and he had a chicken-house. He even had a shed built over the pump so that one could be sheltered from the elements while pumping water. Except for their chicken house, I don't recall that Cheat and Aunt Reldie had any outbuildings. Between their house and Grandpa's was a barn that they would share. Our house did have a front porch but no back porch or outbuildings. Of course, if you have any understanding of country life, you know without my mentioning it that each house had one other smaller but essential outbuilding located at the end of a path some distance from the house.

Our little house (I soon recognized it was pretty small) sat only some fifteen or twenty feet from a dredge ditch that passed behind our back yard. For those who may not know, let me explain what a dredge ditch is and why it was there.

That area of Northwest Tennessee where Broadmoor was located, though some twelve miles from the river, was within the Mississippi's normal flood plain. On our side of the river, for a distance of miles and miles, both north and south, the land's elevation this far from the river was not much higher than at the river's edge. In its natural state, and even after the covering virgin forest was cleared, much of the low-lying land was swampy and untillable. Years before our arrival, to carry away excess water, a system of drainage canals had been excavated. These were called dredge ditches. It was adjacent to one of these that our house was located.

That ditch became the source of a lot of fun and excitement. When we moved there it had water in it year-round and the water was, except in the dryer seasons, clear and clean. Vernon and I, being the only children old enough then, fished in it and would often catch some small catfish or perch. They were small, but they were big enough to eat. After a heavy rain, the ditch would, for a time, run full and, at those times, Vernon and I would bait and set several poles and leave them there overnight. When we checked our poles in the morning we would nearly always find something had been hold of our lines for the tips of our poles would be pulled down into the water. With great expectation, we would pull each one in. On some of them the hook would be empty and bare, all the bait gone. But on a few of them we would almost always find a good-size catfish.

We never did figure out where those larger fish came from after a rain.

That ditch provided us a lot of excitement but the kind of excitement changed with time. Later on, the character of the stream changed. Whereas the water had once been flowing and generally clear, it became murky and still. In the dryer season of summer, although there were deeper pools, much of the length of the ditch was shallow and stagnant. A thick cover of vines, briars and weeds grew along the sides of the ditch and the water could be reached only by the paths we children had trampled out through the brambles.

By this period I speak of, Vernon and I had become friends with all the other local boys and groups of them often visited us. And, while it was strictly forbidden (maybe *because* it was strictly forbidden) we would seek out one of the pools in the ditch and go skinny-dipping. We didn't swim for the water was not deep enough but, at least, we could splash around and get wet.

But there is something else you need to know. That ditch, while it may not have supported many fish, was home to a large population of water moccasins. And when I say large, I mean in both number and size. If we were quiet as we neared the ditch by one of our paths, we would see them laying up on tree branches that hung low over the water. If we came in loud, we would hear them splashing as they hit the water upon our approach.

Common water moccasins, though fearful in appearance, are not poisonous but one variety, the Cottonmouth, is deadly. Fortunately, none of us ever got close enough to any of our snakes to check their identity papers.

Today, you couldn't drag me within yards of that ditch but then we weren't afraid. Not of the snakes, that is, but finally something else scared us away. Once,

Mama's brother, Uncle Moody, came for a visit and he soon caught on to the fact that we were sneaking off and going into the water. A day or so later he took a walk down along the ditch and decided to enter one of our paths to take a look at our swimming hole. As he approached, he disturbed the snakes and, as he later described it, "They sounded like a bunch of fat hogs hitting the water!"

Well, when Moody came back from his walk he didn't mince words. He said it plain and we believed he meant it. If he ever caught us in that ditch again, he wasn't going to tell Mama and he wasn't going to tell Daddy. Instead, he was going to personally beat us to death!

So, at least as long as Moody's visit lasted, we stayed away from the swimming hole.

But we found other recreation that involved the snakes. All us boys carried a slingshot; not a store bought slingshot. We made our own. There were plenty of trees and bushes available so it was no problem finding a suitable forked branch to form the frame. And, at that time, all automobile tires had an inner tube to hold the air and tubes were then made of real rubber; rubber that stretched and popped back briskly when released. We could nearly always salvage a discarded tube that could be cut into narrow strips. Then, we just tied one end of each rubber strip to our frame, fashioned a pocket from the tongue out of an old shoe, attached the pocket to the other end of the rubber strips, and we had ourselves a slingshot.

As ammunition, we used any small, hard object that came to hand. Small rocks were good. Clods of dirt were not so good as they tended to come apart in the air. Sometimes we would find an old piece of cast iron and, by pounding it with a hammer, break it into small pieces. This was the best ammunition of all.

A slingshot was good for taking potshots at most any target but one of the best was a big, fat, sleeping water moccasin. I don't know if we ever killed any but we sure disturbed a lot of their naps.

Before I leave here, I've got to tell one more snake story. One day Mama was on her way to the little house at the end of the path out back when she felt something catch around her ankle. She looked down and saw something green that looked to her like an onion blade. Since the garden was close by, she had no thought that it was anything else. She kicked her foot a couple of times to dislodge it but it continued to cling. Then, as she leaned down to pluck it loose with her hand, she saw that this onion blade had two beady eyes and a forked tongue!

Well, of course, the poor little garden snake was harmless but that didn't dampen Mama's blood-curdling scream. We all came running to see what it was

Mama was about to die of and, when we saw the truth, all had a great laugh; all, that is, but Mama. And the snake, who must have been the most frightened of all.

This is Gene:
Let me interrupt my brother here and introduce a story of my own from the time we lived in the little house on the dredge ditch. I'll tell you about the poke-weed stalk.

Bueford has told you about the dredge ditch that ran behind that house but he hasn't mentioned the dump. Let me explain.

When the drainage ditches he has mentioned were dug, the excavated dirt was dumped alongside the ditch, forming a ridge paralleling it. The ridge was called a ditch dump, or, simply a dump. The width and height of the dump depended, of course, on the amount of excavated dirt. The dump that ran behind our backyard was about six or eight feet high. The slope of the dump, while not precipitous, was fairly steep and, where it wasn't kept trimmed, was covered with a thick growth of weeds and vines. However, Mama and Daddy kept the whole area, the backyard and the portion of the dump that ran behind it, well-trimmed. The dump became a part of the yard.

The first year we lived there I was four years old. I remember that my two older brothers and I liked to play on the dump and I, particularly, liked to climb to the top of the dump and then run down it to the flat yard, reveling in the blinding speed that, it seemed to me, I thereby attained.

One spring a poke-weed sprouted near the bottom of the slope and, for some reason, was allowed to continue to grow. Left alone, a poke-weed will grow into a tough, fibrous stalk that might be some six or eight feet high and with a diameter at the bottom of two or three inches. If it is allowed to mature and dry and is then broken off near the ground, what remains is a jagged stalk of many upward projecting sharp slivers.

In the fall of this particular year our poke-weed had matured and had, in fact, been broken off near the ground leaving a dangerous instrument just lurking there a few inches above ground level, poised to pierce any bare foot or other flesh that came along.

Apparently Mama and Daddy had not noticed the danger.

One warm afternoon I was enjoying my private game of flying off the dump when, as I plunged down it, I stubbed my toe and fell sprawling on my face. And it was my misfortune to land, mouth wide open, squarely upon the up-thrust poke-weed stalk which ripped into the inside of my mouth and throat, doing considerable damage.

As blood began to gush and I began to scream, both Mama and Daddy came running to investigate. Actually, from there I don't have a lot of recall, but Mama remembered. She said Daddy first picked me up, saw the blood pouring from my mouth, and, she said, apparently thinking it was my jugular, "He turned white as a sheet and said to me, he's killed his-self!" Then, she said, he just thrust me into her arms and turned and walked away, leaving her with what she then thought was a dying child in her arms.

Mama was left with no option but to hold on to me and wait for my life's blood to drain away. But, after a while, the flow slowed and it became clear that this was not my time, and all three of us survived. But Mama always remembered the moment as one of stark terror, just like it was yesterday.

14

Broadmoor

This is Bueford again:

I find it difficult to define Broadmoor; to tell you what it was like in such a way that you will understand why, after all these years, it still pulls our minds back to it. As I told you at the beginning, I am not even sure I can understand that myself. But I will try to describe Broadmoor in such a way that you will begin to see.

Broadmoor was a farm, a plantation if you prefer, of maybe two thousand to twenty-five hundred acres. It lay near the northwest corner of Tennessee, astride Highway 78, some four miles south of the small town of Ridgely and twelve miles north of the more substantial town of Dyersburg. The single, most dominating, geographical feature of the area is the Mississippi River which runs about twelve miles to the west of Broadmoor with, at that point, the boot heel of Missouri on the opposite side. The low, rolling hills of Tennessee begin a few miles to the east but Broadmoor is in the lowland, its elevation not many feet above the river's level. For centuries, maybe eons, before the land was developed and protecting levees were built, the entire area was flooded during each high-water season. As each year's floods receded, they left behind the makings of a deep, rich topsoil.

When our family moved to Broadmoor in 1935, and for the entire time we lived there, there were broad fields of cultivated land but there were also large growths, hundreds of acres, of uncut virgin hardwood forest. Great oaks grew there; red oak, white oak, pin oak and others and there was hickory, poplar, ash, elm and many others. In many places groves of cypress still stood, giving evidence of the land's former wet, swampy character.

About six or seven miles to the south, the Obion River flowed in its east to west path past the foot of a line of hills, carrying its water to the Mississippi. Except for the Obion and a few much smaller streams, not large enough to be called rivers, there was no natural drainage for the area.

About fifteen to twenty miles to the north of Broadmoor was Reelfoot Lake which has a rather unique history. Well, I guess what I just said is not entirely true for to say something is unique means it is one of a kind and that is not true of Reelfoot history. The lake has two histories.

The first one, which many prefer to believe, is told in Indian legend. It is the story of a young brave, the only son of a chief of the Chickasaws, who was called Reelfoot. He was called that because of the clubfoot he was given at birth. The young brave, who would one day be chief, was strong and swift as a deer but, when he ran, he swung his clubfoot in an unusual arc and, thus, was given the Reelfoot name.

Now, the time came that his father went to join the spirits of his ancestors and Reelfoot became chief. He was a strong and wise chief but he was lonely, having found none among the young maidens of his own tribe with whom he wished to share his teepee. There was no soft body to warm his blankets at night and no one to tend the corn, dry the venison or chew the deer hides and make them soft.

One night, as Reelfoot pondered his state, he recalled that his father had once told him of a tribe where the young maidens were many and beautiful and skilled in all things that make a teepee a home. This tribe was called the Choctaws and they lived a few days' journey down the river known as The Father of All Waters in a village called Memphis. (I think Memphis, in the Choctaw tongue; means, "Land Where Elvis Walks.")

Taking with him several braves in five canoes, Reelfoot made the journey to Memphis where he was welcomed by the Choctaw chief who invited him to sit by the fire and smoke a pipe. Now, it happened that, as Reelfoot sat there, the fairest of all maidens walked by and he was transfixed by her beauty. When he recovered his faculties, he inquired who she was and learned she was the chief's youngest daughter, Laughing Eyes. Well, Reelfoot, never one to waste the moment, right then began to bargain with the chief for her hand. He offered many baskets of beads and trinkets, bundles of soft, well-chewed skins, three pinto ponies and a five-year lease of hunting rights in the Obion River basin.

Ah, but all Reelfoot's bids and entreaties were rejected. Laughing Eyes' father was adamant. No way he was going to let his daughter marry a clubfoot! So Reelfoot went away without the maiden but he didn't forget her.

He thought about her constantly and, at last, Reelfoot decided he had to have Laughing Eyes, even if he had to steal her, and he began to plan to do that. But one night, as he lay scheming, the Great Spirit came and spoke to him and forbade him to steal the maiden and, seeing Reelfoot wasn't following him, he spelled it out in plain language. The Great Spirit said, if Reelfoot defied him and took the maiden, he would be very angry and he would make the earth to rock and the waters to rush forth and the waters would swallow up, not only Reelfoot, but his entire village and all its people and they would be no more.

Frightened and discouraged, Reelfoot temporarily abandoned any thought of taking the maiden but, at last, there came a time that his love for her exceeded his fear and he knew he had to have her even if it meant incurring the wrath of the Great Spirit. And, besides, surely He wouldn't do what he had threatened.

So it happened that; after the leaves of the trees had fallen and blown away and the first snows had come, he took his most trusted braves and returned down the river. And in the village on the bluffs he crept into Laughing Eyes' tent and gently woke her and, when she saw who it was, she returned his eager embrace but Reelfoot said, "Not right now, Hon." and he wrapped her in his warmest blankets and stole her away in the night.

Overcome by the joy of his conquest, Reelfoot forgot the Great Spirit's promise for a time but when he had gathered together all the village for the wedding festival and while the drums throbbed and there was much dancing and, as Reelfoot savored thoughts of his approaching wedding night, it all came back to him.

Suddenly, in the midst of the celebration, the Great Spirit looked down and said, "I done tried to tell you boy." And he stamped his foot. That's all it took. The earth began to rumble and rock and to rise and fall like an angry sea and smoke spewed from every crevice and the waters flowed forth and all the revelers and the drum beaters and the dancing braves and the maidens and the old and the young and Reelfoot and Laughing Eyes, all of them, were swallowed up and pulled beneath the waters. And they had not even the time to cry out and repent and beg for mercy. All were lost.

After a while the earth ceased its motions and the waters stilled and no sound was heard under the heavens.

Even now, when nights grow long and the hour is late and the stars and a pale moon shine down on the peaceful lake's surface, it is still the same. Except that, once in a while, the Great Spirit is known to lightly put down his foot and make the earth to tremble lest we forget the lesson of Reelfoot and the consequences of disobedience.

But, for the most part, the earth is quiet and the waters are calm and the brave but impatient young chief and his lovely little Laughing Eyes still sleep beneath the beauty of a place called Reelfoot.

I like that explanation of Reelfoot the best but for those who insist that all things move in accordance with laws of physics, this is the scientific explanation.

The great New Madrid fault line runs from the area of the Missouri town of that name, crosses under the Mississippi River and continues on across Lake County, Tennessee. In the winter of 1811–1812 there was a series of earthquakes, including three that are now estimated to have been of a magnitude of eight or more on the Richter scale. During those quakes, large sections of land alternately rose and fell like a surging sea. (as in the Indian legend) One large section of some fifteen thousand acres sank to depths up to twenty feet. The Mississippi flowed backward to fill the depression and that became Reelfoot Lake. Those quakes were felt from the Rocky Mountains to and all up and down the east coast. Boats reportedly foundered in waters at Charleston, South Carolina, and church bells were made to ring in Boston, a thousand miles away.

Since that time there have been hundreds and hundreds of smaller quakes along the fault and experts predict the big one will inevitably come again. They generally predict there is a 90% chance we will see it within the next thirty-five years.

Because the area was sparsely populated in the time of the great quakes, loss of life (except for Reelfoot's tribe) was moderate, but things have changed. The population has vastly grown and, beside numerous smaller ones, there are now two major cities, Memphis and St. Louis, within the area that can be expected to suffer devastating damage.

How bad could it be? Consider this. The 1995 earthquake at Kobe, Japan, which was of a much lesser force, 6.9 on the Richter scale, claimed 5,500 lives and caused one hundred billion dollars in damage.

When the next big one comes here, they say it will be a horror.

But I digress. When our family moved to Broadmoor it had been more than 120 years since the great quakes and they had no effect on our lives beyond their having provided Reelfoot as a popular recreation area. Broadmoor, at the time we moved there, bore no evidence of the quakes beyond, here and there, a few relatively minor depressions that did not appear to be the result of erosion and were probably a lingering result of the quakes.

15

The People: Who They Were; How They Lived.

Recently, my brothers and I, in the course of writing this account, made from memory a rough census of those we could recall who lived at Broadmoor. We came up with a little over two hundred souls; man, woman and child. Actually, that number surprised us. Until we began counting, we wouldn't have guessed there was that many of us. At the end of this chapter, we will provide a list of those we can remember and, later on, will tell you something about some of them.

All these people, except for the farm manager and the storekeeper, lived in tenant houses scattered about the plantation. For the most part the houses were not grouped but sat apart and somewhat distanced from each other, although there were a few groupings, such as the one our family lived in.

With one major exception, that is, the farm manager's residence, all the houses were similar in design and construction. They were all built of rough, unpainted boards. They had no footings or foundations but were set up on blocks hand-sawed out of a felled tree. The walls contained no insulation; the only thing separating the interior from the outside heat or cold being the single thickness of the boards forming the walls and whatever cardboard or wall paper had been applied to the inside. Some floors were made of tongue-and-groove pine but, mostly, they were of plain boards which left cracks through which cold winds blew in winter.

Things like roof lines and porch arrangements varied but, inside, the layout of most was similar and most families used the space in pretty much the same way. The average house had four rooms, all interconnected. There were no hallways or pantries or closets. Hanging and storage space was improvised.

The door used as the front entry led from the porch into the living room in which one would normally find a bed, a small table to hold the Bible and the kerosene lamp that lit the room and one or two rocking chairs and, in cold weather, a heating stove. The stove was taken down in the warm seasons and stored until needed again. In a few houses, one might find a battery-powered radio but they were not common.

In cold weather, the living room was the only one that was heated except the kitchen was heated by the cook stove when it was in use. Typically, the bed in the living room was occupied by the parents of the family. After supper, in the cold seasons, all would gather in the living room around the stove. In warmer times the gathering place was the front porch. There was not much to do except sit and stare at each other and most people were in bed by eight or eight-thirty. Some of the older children might sit up later reading or playing exciting games like Rook or Chinese checkers.

Except for the entry, there would be two doors in the living room; one opening into the kitchen/eating area and one into the room on the other front corner of the house.

This latter room would be used as a bedroom and would usually contain at least two beds. There was little other furniture here and none that was not essential. In most houses, this room also had a door opening onto the front porch.

The other door from the living room led into the kitchen/eating room where there would be a wood burning cook stove, an eating table covered with oilcloth and whatever number of mismatched table chairs or stools as the family required. There would be a washstand, generally hand made, near the back door. On it would stand the water bucket which held about two gallons of water brought in from the pump outside. A dipper rested in the bucket and, when anyone was thirsty, they dipped up a quantity of water from the bucket and drank from the dipper. (If the drinker did not completely empty the dipper, it was not considered polite to empty the excess water back into the bucket. The thoughtful person stepped to the back door and tossed the surplus water out on the ground.)

Setting beside the water bucket was a wash pan; a shallow, metal basin used for washing face and hands. One might use the cool water from the water bucket or, if he preferred, the warm water from the kettle or reservoir of the cook stove. (The typical wood burning cook stove had a compartment, called the reservoir, mounted near the firebox and designed to hold water that would be kept warm when there was a fire in the stove.) When one was finished with his ablutions, he, also, would step to the back door and toss the used wash water out onto the ground. Also, probably hanging on a nail, there would be a larger pan used to wash the dishes. The water used came from the same source and, when the chore was finished, was disposed of in the same way. The kitchen would also contain a flour barrel, a suitable container for the corn meal and another for the dried beans, and a stand of lard. In some corner would be the pie safe. And there would be such hand-built shelves or racks as the resident had devised for other storage.

The other room on a back corner of a house would, if needed, be used as another bed room. Else, it would probably be used for miscellaneous storage.

There would be a back porch and, either on it or near it, hanging on nails driven into the wall, would be two or three wash tubs and the rub-board. Sitting in the back yard would be the large, black wash pot used to boil clothes on wash day. Together, the tubs, pot and rub-board were the equivalent of today's automatic washer. A line strung between two posts or trees was the dryer. (In a recent discussion, Lynn reported an article he had just seen that amused him. It described a similar device, touted as a new idea, called a solar clothes dryer.)

Somewhere in most back yards was a chicken house. Inside it, a few feet off the ground, was mounted a series of roost poles. This is where the chickens spent the night. Each evening, about dusk, they would begin gravitating to the chicken house where they would, one by one, hop up and take their place on a roost pole and settle in. Later, if one should look into the chicken house, he would find all the chickens lined up side by side on the roost poles and there they would remain until the following dawn.

One other essential structure was the family outhouse. We will say no more about that than necessary.

Some of the tenant houses were smaller and were laid out differently but their contents were similar.

There was one house on Broadmoor that was different than all the others. It was, in comparison with them, huge. It sat back some fifty yards off the main road and it was built of finished lumber and painted white. It had two stories and had broad halls and stairways and ten-foot ceilings. A wide veranda ran across the front and down one side.

I don't know when the house was built, or by whom, but it was in first-rate condition when we lived at Broadmoor. There was one thing about the house that I now think was odd. Although it was plain no expense was spared in its construction, there was no indoor plumbing and I wonder why some provision wasn't made for that.

When we first moved to Broadmoor a Mr. Bully Thurman lived there. (I don't know if Bully was his real name or he was just called that.) but he moved away not long after we arrived. About that time, Mr. Sam Fussell became the farm manager (We called him the straw boss.) and he and his family moved in.

As the rest of us became acquainted with the Fussell kids we were allowed, in fact welcomed, to visit and, thus we became familiar with the interior. I think what most impressed me then was the attic. It seemed to me it offered unlimited space to be explored and to be hid in when we played hide and seek.

Structures on Broadmoor, in addition to the tenant houses and the one big house I have described, included the store, the several barns and storage sheds and three churches. There was a Southern Baptist church, called Bruce's Chapel, the Church of Christ, and another, not identified with a specific denomination, attended by the black people, commonly called, in that time, Colored Folks (and often by a less palatable name). The Colored church also served as a school building for the black kids.

What follows is a list, to the best of our collective memory, of persons who lived at Broadmoor while we did. (Also on the list are few who lived at Cuckleburr, some of whom became important to our story.) They are listed in no particular order; rather just as they came to mind. Some names are duplicated, being listed, first, with their parents and, later, in their own household. While we tried, we don't guarantee all names are spelled correctly.

Waltie Kennedy. He was married to Hester Nale and they had two daughters, Metha and Sue.

Mr. L.M. Dudley, married to Novell. The family included two daughters, Donnie and Faye; and one son, Wallace.

Wallace Dudley. Married to Helen. Their children are Freeman, Joe, Bobby, Wallace, Paul, Roger and Patricia.

Ralph Eaton was married to Sophia McDaniel and they had three sons, Carlton, Billy and Gaythal. His father, first name unknown, lived in a separate household with Ralph's brother, Ellis, and two sisters, one of whom was Travis who later became the second wife of Millard Parker.

Thomas McDaniel and his wife, Julia, were mostly just called "Mac" and "Miss Mac." Their daughters were Lorene, Irene, Sophia, Katherine and Mildred; and their sons were JT and Shirley.

Floyd Johnson was married to Irene McDaniel. They had no children.

Rube Cherry was married to Millie. A granddaughter Pearl, lived with them. Pearl later married Bud Fussell. He had another granddaughter, Bonnie.

Sam Fussell and his wife, Pearl Putman; had daughters Hazel, Melvina (called Sis) and Peggy; and sons Calvin (called Bud) and Samuel J. (called Bo). Hazel and Sis married non-local men. Peggy married me, Bueford Weaver. Bo married

Marcene Robison, daughter of Jack and Flossie and Bud married the Cherry granddaughter, Pearl.

Jim Johnson and his wife, Preble, had a large family including daughters, Charlene, Pam-Ellie (possibly Pamela), Virginia, Maud, Maxine and Nazalene and, sons. Willard, (called Hunt), Millard (called Fatty), Leland (called Pee Wee) and Bonnie Dillard. Willard later married Dorothy Nale.

Clyde Green first married Annie Lou and they had daughters. Virginia, Christine, Lois and Joyce, and a son called Buddy. Mrs. Annie Lou later died in a house fire and Clyde married again to a Mrs. James, who had a son, William, whom we called, humorously, Perchworthy)

Roe Green and his wife, Anna Mae, had sons, Melvin and Carmel.

James Sellers and Lena had daughters Dorothy and Gertrude and sons, David (called Red), Gene Autry, and Glendel.

Barlow and Etta Parker; had sons, Millard, William (called wick), Doots (real name unknown), Cletus, Royce, and Don.

Millard Parker first married Maggie Lay and they had children, Odie, Joe and Modine. Maggie died of tuberculosis and he later married Travis Eaton.

William (Wick) Parker was married to Louise. Their children are Nora Nell, Quanita, William Earl, Shirley, Larry Joe, Odell and Janice.

Cletus Parker. Was married to Alberta. Their children were Shirley and Gail.

Oce Wolf and Miss Myrtle (a Buchanan); had daughters, Sudie and Mary, and sons, Lonnie, Junior and Johnny.

Ed Nale was married to Nettie and they had daughters, Hester, Bernice, Dorothy, Elizabeth, Rachael and Hazel and sons, Woodrow and Homer. Hester married Waltie Kennedy, who became our storekeeper; Rachel married Jessie Lay of Cuckleburr, Dorothy married Willard Johnson

Rex Thurmon and Vallie had a daughter, Edith, who married Calvin Pilkenton, and another, Flossie, who married Jack Robison.

Austin Thurmon and spouse had a daughter, Alavern, and possibly one other, and a son, T.C.

Slim Henderson, (real name unknown) and his wife, Catherine, had a daughter, Lurlene, who married Walter (Shorty) Gregory of Cuckleburr, and sons, Harvey Ray and Billy Joe. Later, they informally adopted Oren Bissell.

Jack Robison and Flossie had daughters, Marcene, Sharon, Sonya, the twins, Sherly and Cheryl and a son called Bubba.

K.P. Lay and Ruby (a Garrison) had two daughters, Helen and Carol and a son, Bryant.

Bill Lay and Eloise (pronounced E-Lois) had a son Billy.

"**Uncle" Dootsie Walls.** Wife was maybe Aunt Suzie.

Spence Lay; married Irma Thurkiel. We don't recall any children.

W.B. Simpson, was the storekeeper before Waltie Kennedy. He and his wife, whose name we don't recall, had no children.

Grady Buchanan; and his wife, Loe (phonetic spelling) had a daughter, Darlene; and sons, J.C. and Gerald. Grady was a brother to Mrs Myrtle Wolf and Mrs. Rosie Pilkenton.

Riley Buchanan; and Lillie (Waltie Kennedy's sister) had a son, Sammy. (We won't tell you what his mother called Sammy as a baby, a name that some still call him.)

William A. (Bill) Weaver;(our grandpa) and his wife, Cassie Craig, had a daughter, Arelda, and sons Rufus (our daddy) and Woodrow (called Dirk)

James Rufus Weaver;(Our daddy) We will tell you elsewhere of his children and marriages.

Cheatham Tidwell married Arelda Weaver and they had no children

Woodrow (Dirk) Weaver married Ernestine Pilkenton; daughter of Stoney and Rosie Pilkenton, and they had a son, Everett; and daughters, Patricia (called Pat) and Gloria

Mr. Reeves (first name not recalled), married Mossie; and had sons Arthur Lee and Tim

Alvin McElrath; married Narcissis (called Sister). They had no children; although Alvin is believed to have had children living elsewhere.

Paul Sampson and Mittie had no children that we know of.

Booker (last name and spouse's name uncertain) had sons, John Lee, Isom and Ocie B.

The Duff family included a girl, Helen, and a boy, Junior. We don't recall the parents' names.

Stoney Pilkenton and Rosie had sons, Calvin and Buford, and two daughters, Ernestine and Peggy.

Henry Green. (Father of Clyde and Roe) was the mule wrangler at Broadmoor.

Bowd Matheney and Cora had a daughter, Carly.

Mr. and Mrs. Williams, first names unknown, had a son, Robell.

Mace Robinson and Flora had a son, Yvonne (pronounced wye-von) and daughters, Evonne and Katherine. Katherine, called Cacky, married Hub Henderson and Yvonne, after they moved away to Chicago, married Gertrude Sellers and we believe they had several children.

L. C. Howie; married Sudie Wolf and they had a daughter, Sylvia, and a son, Ronnie.

Rosie Hood had sons, Clifford and Ozell

Ted Roberson, married Virginia Johnson. We believe they have a daughter, Sue.

Jim Garrison, and his wife, Ollie Bee, had children, Bobby, Shelby, Barbara and Janice. (Jim was a brother to Ruby who married K. P. Lay.)

Mr. Coats, first name and history unknown, was a bee keeper and associate of our daddy. His home was in Tiptonville but, for a while, he lived near us in a hand-built mobile home.

The Thurkiel Family (spelling phonetic) included several children, one of which was a boy, Reilly (also phonetic). Reilly married Mary Lee Short of Cuckleburr.

We also list some remembered classmates from the Cuckleburr school who lived elsewhere than Broadmoor

The Lays, children of Dan and Myrtle, lived at Cuckleburr. There was a boy, Purvis, a girl, Dorothy, then two sets of twins, each set a girl and a boy, Cleo and Leo and Bessie and Jessie. Jessie married Rachel Nale. We think Mr. Lay was a brother to Bill and K.P. and, possibly to Spence.

The Boswell Kids lived at Cuckleburr. We don't recall the parents' names but the children were the girls, Lois, Lavern, Louise and Mary Ruth and the boys, Glenn, Delbert and Bobby (called Fish)

The Short girls, Mary Lee and Gracie Ruth.

John and Martin Ayres

Joe, Rupert and Orland Heathcott

Ralph Sanford

Marvin Foster

Junior Hubble

Barbara, Jere and Carol Strachn

Walter Gregory

Raymond and Freeman Kemp, and sisters, names we don't recall.

16

The Work

Everyone on Broadmoor worked, with the exception of very young children and the old and infirm. There were several families, including ours, who rented or share-cropped portions of the Broadmoor plantation and were, therefore, self-employed. Most of the land, however, was leased by one individual, Mr. Jack Bratton, who hired the major portion of the Broadmoor population to work for him as day laborers.

As we reflect, now, we see this might have been a part of the reason that Broadmoor exuded a different atmosphere. At other places we lived, we were surrounded by smaller, family owned and operated farms. While those families were our neighbors, and, for the most part, our friends, they didn't depend on us or we on them. Each was independent. At Broadmoor, on the other hand, the majority of the populace not only lived near each other, they worked side by side every day for the same master and each contributed to the success or failure of the operation that provided sustenance to them all.

While we in our family had our own farms to tend, we often worked with them and we shared school, store, churches and recreation and became as much a part of Broadmoor as any who worked and lived there. Perhaps this was a part of the cement that bound us together.

As we go forward, we will refer to the major operation as "Broadmoor Farms." Mr. Bratton was commonly called "Captain Jack" which was, we understand, some acknowledgment of his army service in World War I. On any day that farm work was being done you would likely see him driving among the fields in his car. I don't recall that I ever saw him dismount from the car and he only spoke to his farm manager, "Mr. Sam."

When we first moved to Broadmoor there was no mechanization; no tractors. The work of pulling the plows and other farming implements was done by mules and a large number of them were required. Each renter or sharecropper had a team of two, but Broadmoor Farms utilized at least twenty or twenty-five teams, a total of some forty or fifty mules.

One of the local characters was Mr. Henry Green, the one who was responsible for feeding the mules every day. He lived in a house down behind the mule lot. Though apparently in good health, he was somewhat elderly and no longer capable of doing a full day of ordinary farm labor. But the job he had wasn't easy. Considerable effort was required to keep close to twenty-five tons of mule-flesh fed and watered each day. (Figure it out: say fifty mules averaging out at near a thousand pounds each.)

Mr. Green was a jolly old fellow; always whistling as he went about his work. He could whistle loud but he also tended to whistle unintentionally when he talked, probably because of some malformation of his teeth. He liked to make a joke out of it, deliberately using words with a sibilant sound. He would tell his audience, "I'm going to have sssalmon and sssoup for sssupper!" Then he would laugh like he had just told a knee-slapper.

It was always somewhat of a mystery to me how the mule drivers, some twenty or twenty-five of them, could walk out each morning into that passel of mules and, unfailingly, pick out their own team. But they did.

A mule is not a handsome animal but they will work hard all day long and, in the hands of a skilled driver, will do what is asked of them. Usually, all the mule teams used by Broadmoor Farms would work in the same field, performing whatever task was at hand, and finish that operation before moving on to the next. That put a lot of mule teams in the same place at the same time and could, if not organized, have led to confusion. But the drivers took pride in their ability to maintain their precise position with respect to one another. If they were cultivating cotton, for instance, the first team in line would start down a row. When he was about a mule-length ahead, the next would fall in line in the next row. And the next would follow him, and the next would take his proper place, and so on until the entire group was moving across the field in echelon formation at the same speed and at the same interval of separation. Seen from a distance, they appeared to move with the precision of a troop of cavalry passing in review.

The farm work day in that time was typically from six to six with a break for the noon meal, called dinner, and, maybe, a couple of shorter breaks at "quartering time," that is, at mid-morning and mid-afternoon. On the average, farm workers put in ten or more hours of work each day.

Let's do a little arithmetic. Say a mule driver, in one work day, walked ten hours behind his mules traveling at two miles per hour (a conservative estimate), he would cover twenty miles. And he would do this while walking on soft, uneven soil and all the while constantly guiding the cultivating plows and directing his team. Imagine the stamina required to do this every day for weeks on end! At the time I'm speaking of, the drivers' pay was probably no more than a dollar and a half a day. Put another way, that's fifteen cents an hour or seven and a half cents per mile. And they were glad to get the work.

(Lynn recalls a young man, working as a general laborer but occasionally assigned to fill in as a mule driver, who, like one who saw his life's goal within reach, was heard to remark proudly, "I think by this time next year I'll have my own team!")

All other members of Broadmoor families; men, women and children, except those that were very old or very young, found plenty work to keep them busy. One of their jobs was chopping cotton during the growing season, and there was plenty cotton to chop; lots and lots of cotton; hundreds of acres of cotton. And every acre, every row, of it had to be chopped at least three times in the growing season.

Cotton, in that era, was planted so that the seedlings, when they first appeared, formed a solid row with no interval between plants. But cotton plants won't produce that way. They need room to grow and for the branches to spread. So, during the first chopping, the plants had to be thinned so that no more than one or two plants remained in a clump with the clumps several inches apart. And any ground that will grow cotton will also grow grass and weeds and they had to be cleaned out, else they would retard the growth of the emerging plants. Today there is machinery and chemicals to thin the plants and kill the weeds but, in our time, the only machinery available to us was a hoe and the only chemical was our sweat.

Most of the weeds and grass that grew in the furrows between the rows of cotton was removed by a cultivator's plows but the plows could not be allowed to get too close to the plants as that could cause damage to the roots. Thus, the cultivator would leave an untouched strip of earth several inches wide, with the row of cotton plants running down the middle. It was the chopper's job, with his hoe, to chop or scrape away any weeds or grass that grew among the cotton plants in this strip.

In the second and third choppings there might be stretches of a few feet where no weeds grew and the chopper could pick up his hoe and walk ahead to the next place where a stroke was required. But, for the first chopping, because of the thinning required, every single foot of each row required at least a couple of strokes. Over a ten-hour work day that could add up to a lot of strokes.

Cotton choppers were paid by the day. I have no clear recollection of the standard daily wage when we first moved to Broadmoor in the thirties, but it was probably no more than a dollar a day for adults and less than that for us kids.

Chopping cotton was hard work but probably the hardest work done on Broadmoor Farms was putting out tomato plants. While our family was not directly employed by Broadmoor Farms, we took advantage of any opportunity to earn some extra cash money so we, us kids at least, always helped set tomato plants.

We would plant large fields, forty of fifty acres in a plot. Once the ground was prepared to receive the plants, it was marked off in grids by pulling a piece of wheeled machinery across the soft earth, making parallel tracks. Then, the same implement would be pulled across the same ground at a ninety degree angle to the first, thus marking out neat grids. One plant would then be set at each intersection of the lines.

Sounds easy, don't it? Well, wait a minute.

The actual planting was done by two-person teams, one adult and one young person. The adult carried an ordinary spade and held it so that its broad dimension was parallel to the row to be planted. He would jab the point of the spade into the dirt. (The loose dirt offered little resistance) and immediately pull the handle across his chest which opened a slit in the dirt behind the blade. Simultaneously with the opening of the hole, the younger member of the team, who had stooped for that purpose, thrust a tomato plant in it. The adult then, with one smooth motion, placed a foot on the dirt in front of the blade, rocked the spade handle back, closing the opening into which the plant had been placed and pulled the spade free while the pressure of his foot pressed the dirt down firmly on the roots of the plant and the plant was set.

The adult then took one or two paces forward and repeated the process.

For the young person, the day was a constant exercise of stoop, place a plant, stand up, move two steps, stoop, place a plant, and that continued all day. It wasn't hard work for the adult member of the team but, for the young person, it was back-breaking. I doubt that an adult, being less supple, could have held out at that for very long.

Once they established a rhythm, the team could move across the field with a pace comparable to a slow stroll. We kids were thankful that this operation usually lasted only a few days and we could return to the less rigorous work of chopping cotton.

Farmers of that era strove to be "laid by" by the fourth of July. Laying by, or being laid by, meant all the hard work of nurturing the growing cotton crop was done and they had only to wait for the harvest which would begin around the first of September.

That was cotton-pickin' time. That time was much welcomed by the farmer who, as the cotton was gathered and sold, would finally see some cash return on the hard labor and money he had invested, but, for day-laborers like us, it meant even more. It was a time we had looked toward all year. For all the other months we worked for a bare-subsistence daily wage which, no matter how hard we worked, could not be stretched. But, at cotton picking, when we would be paid, not by the day, but for the pounds we picked, we could set our own wage.

It would wound me deeply, now, to know my wife and my children had to go to the fields and labor all day long under a blazing sun as my mother and my brothers did but, in the days of my youth, in the society into which we were born, there was no other option.

As I look back, I marvel that children of my time did not whine or complain or lament their station in life. But they didn't. From their earliest years, they knew nothing awaited them but a life of labor and, when the time came to shoulder their burden, they embraced it eagerly.

I still have a vivid memory of one of the proudest days of my life. It was not a day that I caught an impossible pass or got the game-winning hit or swished the net for three at the buzzer and was mobbed by the student body. It was much more important than that.

It was the first time I ever made a whole dollar in one day!

That season they were paying a dollar per hundred for picking cotton and I had been getting close to a hundred pounds a day and was improving each week. We normally went to the fields early and stayed late. One day when I weighed up with the sun already sinking behind the trees, I was just a few pounds short of a hundred for the day and I wanted that so bad! Some resolve was born inside me and I knew this was the day. I wanted that hundred pounds and I meant to get it.

I told Mama that she and the rest of the kids should go on to the house and I was going back to get what I lacked. Like mamas are supposed to do, she said the other kids could go on but she would come back and help me so it wouldn't take so long. But I declined. I knew, for it to have meaning, this was a line I had to cross alone. On one side of it there was a child but on the other side there was a Boy!

I think Mama instinctively saw where I stood and she took the kids and left me and I went back and, alone there in the gathering dusk, I did it. I got my hundred pounds.

A day like that a man doesn't forget. A part of me will always be that proud and happy boy who had, that day, just earned his first whole dollar.

17

When Cotton Was King

I have already talked some about cotton farming and will talk more about it as we go along. I realize that many who read this, having had no personal involvement with it, may not understand what I am talking about. Perhaps some background would be helpful.

I write of a time when Cotton ruled the south. It was the main money crop. It was what put food on the table and clothes on the back and made it possible for Southern farm folk to survive. A few prospered but, mostly, they just survived. Farmers grew other crops, particularly corn to feed their livestock, but that was just as a sideline to cotton.

Some larger operators had found a market for other crops and they diversified. I have mentioned tomatoes grown at Broadmoor. There was another producer, Mr. Puckett, who farmed large expanses in the Cat Corner community, some three or four miles east of Broadmoor. Every spring he would plant a hundred or more acres of radishes. The growing and harvest season for them was such that it did not interfere with cotton farming. In the spring many of us from Broadmoor, and hundreds of others from around the area, would descend on the radish fields and, for a few days, earn some extra cash money.

The radishes were laid out in beds about six feet wide where they were planted in rows, cross-wise of the bed, the rows being some four to six inches apart. When harvesting the radishes (We called it "pulling" them) the harvester, down on his knees, would crawl along the bed and pull the radishes that were mature enough and tie them in bunches of ten or twelve using rubber bands or lengths of twine. He pulled a bushel basket along with him to put his bunches in and, when the basket was full, he shouldered it and carried it to a tallying station where his bunches were counted and he was paid, on the spot, at something like a nickel a bunch. It was dirty but not difficult work and provided a pleasant respite from our other labors.

But I started out to talk about cotton. Cotton was, undeniably, The King. He was commonly depicted in cartoons as a jolly, smiling, Old-King-Cole kind of character but, in reality, he was a harsh and demanding master, requiring of his subjects complete subjugation and long days of rigorous labor. For that they reaped scant reward.

The process of growing cotton began with the preparation of the ground and that began, if cotton was grown on the plot the previous year, with stalk cutting. The old, empty stalks from the last season were tough and fibrous and stood anywhere from two or three feet to five or six feet high. They had to be reduced to matter that could be assimilated into the soil. This was done with a stalk cutter.

The operative part of the stalk cutter was a sort of reel, maybe two feet in diameter, with laterally mounted blades, placed about six inches apart around the circumference. The reel looked a little like an enlarged blade from a reel-type lawn mower. As the cutter was pulled down a row of stalks, it would first push the stalks over and then, as the reel rolled over them, the blades would chop them into short lengths. The reel was mounted between two wheels. There was a wooden tongue projecting forward as a part of the hook-up to the two mules that pulled it. Above the reel there was a seat for the driver.

Stalk cutting, while time consuming, was not hard work, except maybe for the mules. But it was cold work, done mostly in the winter and the worst part was when some of the debris picked up by the blades would fly up and hit the driver's cold ears. That could smart.

The arduous work began in the spring when it became time to start preparing the soil to receive the seeds. There were three steps, although one might skip one of the steps if he believed he could properly prepare the soil without it.

The first step was called "breaking" the ground and that was done with a turning plow. This plow had a point that dug into the soil and, flaring out on the right side, a broad, curving blade shaped so that, as it was drawn along, it loosened a strip of soil, about six to eight inches wide, turned it over, and left it laying, partially upside down.

The tongue of the plow was attached by a clevis to the double tree, to which was hooked the two single trees, one behind the heels of each mule. The trace chains, hooked behind to the single trees, were fed through the back band, which kept the chains from drooping when slack, and were attached, in front, to the hames which were fitted against the padded collar the mule wore around his neck. Thus, the pressures of pulling the plow, or whatever other implement the mule was pulling, were born by the padded collar.

At the rear of the plow were the handles which the plowman used to control it. By pushing the handles to one side or the other, he could change the plow's direction. If he wanted his plow to go deeper, he lifted the handles which caused the plow point to dig in. If he wanted to plow more shallowly, he pushed down on the handles, raising the point. Normally, the earth was turned to a depth of four to six inches.

To direct the mules, the plowman used voice commands; "Gee" and they would go right; "Haw" and they would go left and, of course, they responded to "Whoa" and Get-up." If he needed more control, he had the reins (We called them plow lines) that were attached to the bits in the mules' mouths. Since his hands were too busy to hold the lines individually, they were tied together and looped over one shoulder then behind the back and under the other arm. This way he could, as needed, reach out and pull on one line or the other. After a round or two, the mule on the right would be walking in plowed ground and the other on unplowed ground. For the most part, they knew their job and could be depended upon to walk a straight line and needed little direction.

NOTE: Contrary to what was depicted in a modern, well-regarded movie, the heroine was not required to walk in front and lead the mules across the field.

Plow time was a good time. Days were growing longer and warmer. A little green was beginning to show in the trees. Birds were on the wing and hungry for the fat earthworms left wriggling behind the plow. The gray, dreary days of winter were past and there was an exciting sense in the air of new beginnings.

For a farm child, one of early spring's great pleasures was running along behind a turning plow, feeling the warm softness of the new-turned earth on his bare feet, while he inhaled its rich aroma and while the soft plodding sound of the mules' hooves and the creaking of the harness and the subtle, muffled snapping of roots and vines broken by the plow fell upon his ears.

The second step in soil preparation was disking. A disk, as you might guess, was an implement made up of gangs of round, sharp, blade-like components mounted on a common axel. It was pulled across the ground with the gangs of disks set at a slight angle to the line of travel. This caused them to cut into the earth and made them rotate so that the top few inches of the earth was cut loose and thrust aside. Trailing gangs of disks were set at an opposite angle so the dirt, picked up by the front gangs and tossed one way, was again picked up and thrown the opposite direction, helping to break up any clods or lumps.

The third step was harrowing. A harrow is a wide, flat, ground-hugging implement with dozens of down-pointed prongs which, when dragged across the ground, further pulverizes the soil.

Once all this was done, some farmers, preferring to plant their crop on a ridge, employed another plow, called a "middle buster." A middle buster was very similar to a turning plow except it had a flaring blade on each side, not just one. As it was pulled along, it threw the soil out in both directions. When a series of passes were made, it produced a field of furrows and ridges.

Now, the soil fully prepared, the farmer was ready to plant his crops and, for that, he used still another implement, a planter, usually one that planted two rows at a time. On the planter were hoppers in which the seeds were placed. At the bottom of the hopper was an adjustable rotating mechanism geared to the wheels which could be set to dispense the desired number of seeds at the desired interval. At ground level there was a small, narrow plow that, as the planter moved along, opened a little trench in the soil. When dispensed from the hopper, the seeds fell through a tube and into the trench. Then, as the planter moved on, the loose dirt fell back and covered the seeds and the seeds were planted.

If the planted crop was cotton, and if the weather cooperated, the farmer would soon, at long last, have a field of emerging cotton plants ready to chop.

We have already discussed the chopping and cultivating of the cotton from this point. Now let me tell you about cotton pickin' as it was done in the time of my youth.

Cotton, as we have discussed, was planted in rows. In harvest time, all the pickers began on one side of the field and, each taking one or two rows at a time, worked their way across it until all the field was completely picked. Mostly, only the younger pickers took one row. Most adults preferred to take two. Once a picker began a row, it was his and he was expected to finish it before going to the next.

When taking two rows, the picker would first pick all the cotton from the stalks on one row for a distance of two or three feet and then would swing to the other row and do the same. He would continue down his rows in that manner.

A cotton plant, as it grows, produces pods, dozens of them, which contain the cotton. These pods are called bolls and that is pronounced like "bowls", not balls. In late August the bolls begin to mature and the outer covering, the hull, cracks open, exposing the fiber inside. The fiber, wet in the closed boll, now dries and fluffs out and is ready to pick. By the first of September, usually, enough of the cotton has opened to begin picking.

Not all the bolls open at the same time; some continuing to open on into the late fall. In modern times, with fast-moving mechanical pickers available, a farmer can wait until it is all open and pick it all with one operation. But, in the days of hand-picking, he could not do that. He had to pick what he could when he could. Over the season, pickers would pass through the fields at least three times in order to harvest all the cotton.

In each boll, the cotton fiber is divided into four or five sections called locks. To withdraw the cotton from the hull, that is to pick it, one grasps the cotton so that a finger closes on each lock and he plucks it out. A good picker does this cleanly in one motion so that he does not have to return to the same boll a second time. When he has picked one boll of cotton, and while reaching for the next, his fingers push it toward the back of his hand where he lightly grips it in his partially closed palm, leaving his fingers free to grasp the cotton in the next boll. In this way he can accumulate four or five bolls of cotton in each hand before he has to interrupt his rhythm and transfer all the cotton to one hand and, with that hand, reach back and deposit it into his sack.

The sack the picker wears has an attached strap that is looped over a shoulder in such a manner that the mouth hangs open beside his hip. Knowing where the sack's mouth is, and accustomed to doing it, the picker drops the cotton in the sack without having to look at what he is doing.

While the one hand is depositing the picked cotton into the sack, the picker's other hand is already reaching for the next boll. In this way, he moves across the field with both hands in constant motion.

Cotton sacks came in standard lengths of seven and a half or nine feet. Most serious pickers used the nine foot sack which allowed them to empty up less often, thus saving time. Depending on the moisture content of the cotton, a nine foot sack might hold as much as eighty-five pounds; however, most preferred to empty their sack sooner as some considerable energy was required to continue dragging that weight across the ground.

Any time he chose, however, the picker could pick up his sack, throw it across his shoulder, and carry it to the scales provided by the farmer. There the cotton was weighed and recorded to the picker's account. The picker threw his full sack up into the farmer's wagon or trailer, climbed up behind it, and emptied it. (If any ladies or small children were weighing up at the same time, it was considered polite for men or boys to empty their sacks for them.)

The picker carried his empty sack back to the same rows he had left and resumed picking. And he did this day in and day out, ten and twelve hours a day, for as long as there was cotton to pick, usually on into late November. On Saturday, the farmer would pay the pickers according to the total, in pounds, of the cotton they had picked since the last pay day. I have picked cotton for less than a dollar a hundred but, as war time (that is WW II) prices increased, I eventually earned as much as four or four-fifty per hundred.

As a minimum, most adults, or adolescent children, could pick around two hundred pounds in a day. Many, however, could pick three hundred to three-fifty. It was the unusual picker that picked four hundred and the very rare that could get five hundred.

As the year drew to a close, with winter coming on, the fields were nearly stripped and the only cotton left was in partially-opened bolls that could not be picked in the normal manner. Still, there was some value in the cotton. For a much-reduced per-pound rate, those who were hardy enough could go back and gather this cotton (We called that "pulling"). In doing this, no effort was made to separate the cotton from the hulls. The bolls, hulls and all, were pulled from the stalk.

Pulling cotton was the last chance to make any money before cotton chopping time next spring. By the time it came to this, we kids would be back in school so we would go out on Saturdays to earn what we could. Pulling cotton was hard. The ground was usually muddy and, if it wasn't, it was because it was frozen. The icy winds blew and, while, for this work we could wear gloves, our hands and feet knew the cold.

What kept us going was the knowledge that the work would soon be done and that what we were earning was going to be our Christmas money.

Through the harvest season our family picked a lot of cotton but none of it was ours so we were not involved in the marketing but, briefly, this is how the system operated. Ginning was the process by which the seeds imbedded in the cotton were separated from the fiber. In the cotton-growing South, there was always a gin within a reasonable distance of any grower. When we were at Broadmoor the closest gin was at Bogota, some four miles away. In the early years Grandpa Weaver, and most farmers, transported the cotton to the gin in a mule-drawn wagon. With some packing and tromping, a wagon could be made to hold the necessary volume of cotton (about 1600 to 2000 pounds) to produce a bale. An average bale of ginned cotton weighed about five hundred pounds. In later years, after he acquired a car to pull it with, Grandpa used a rubber-tired trailer.

The seed from the ginned cotton could be processed to produce cotton seed oil so they had a value. The ginner would usually accept the seed as his fee for ginning the cotton.

As each bale of cotton was ginned, a small sample was pulled from it and this was used to assign a grade, or a quality, to the cotton in the bale. I never fully understood the grading system but representative grades might be middling, low middling, strict low middling, and so on. The grade assigned determined the price paid for the cotton. A representative of the gin usually functioned as a broker and bought the baled cotton on the spot.

In those days, farmers like Grandpa Weaver, who owned their farming equipment and livestock but not the land, paid the land owner for its use with a share of the crops produced. For cotton, the standard payment of the time was one third. The broker had prior knowledge of this arrangement. Thus, when Grandpa took a load of cotton to the gin, the broker would write him a check for two thirds of its value and would hold the land-owner's share under some kind of trust agreement.

Before we leave the subject of hard, back-breaking farm labor, let me tell you something about corn. Corn, in our part of the country, was not generally grown as a cash crop; only as a means of providing food for the livestock. The land for planting corn was prepared in the same way as for cotton, but the growing corn required less care and did not have to be chopped like cotton. Using a cultivator, the furrows were plowed out once or twice to take out most of the weeds and to loosen the soil but, early in the year, when the stalks were knee-high or so, the corn was considered laid by.

It was in the gathering season that corn got its revenge for having been neglected. Mostly, while the weather was good, all hands were concentrating on harvesting cotton, the cash crop. Corn was left standing in the fields until the rain and the mud and the cold weather arrived. (Again, since a boy was needed, a boy who was most likely, by that time, back in school, most of this work was done on a Saturday.) Pulling corn required, in addition to the mules and wagon, a team of three, including the boy. Each pass through the field took five rows. One puller on each side was responsible for gathering the ears of corn from two standing rows and tossing it into the wagon. Normally, except for wading through the mud, this wasn't such hard work. Late in the season, with the stalks brittle, most ears could be snapped free in one quick, twisting, one-handed motion.

The hardest job, always assigned to the boy, was the down-row. The wagon, as it passed through the field, had to straddle one row and it left the cornstalks laying on the ground. That's why it was called the down-row. The adults, forgetting whatever youthful experience they had, took the attitude that, since the boy on the down-row had to pull only half as much corn, his job was easy. They forgot that every ear of corn he pulled was from a broken down stalk so that he was constantly stooping. And, since he had to wait until the wagon had passed to reach any corn at all, he was always behind.

Now, with this brief explanation, I will leave the subject of corn but I feel obligated to offer this bit of free advice. As you go through life, seize opportunity as it comes but never, ever accept a position that requires you to take the down-row.

18

School Days

Soon after our family moved to Broadmoor and got settled in, Vernon and I were ready to enter school (Gene was still too young) but we found there was no school at Broadmoor. We had to go to the school in the Cuckleburr community, a mile or so south of Broadmoor. We later learned the real name of the school was Mitchell but that name was not posted anywhere. In everyone's mind, it was the Cuckleburr School.

It might be well to take a moment or two to explain what cuckleburr means. Mainly, for a farmer in the South, it means trouble. There is a mean, prolific and almost indestructible weed that grows there, called a cocklebur. We natives corrupted that and called it a cuckleburr. A cuckleburr could grow taller, wider, thicker and faster than the cotton or corn it insisted on mingling with. You chop it out, turn your back, and there it is again; hogging the sunlight and the nutrients from the ground.

But it was more than just an offensive weed. It was an *intelligent*, offensive weed. It planned and executed its own distribution system. Each plant, if allowed to mature, produced what seemed like thousands of seed pods and they didn't just fall to the ground and lay there waiting to sprout next spring. They traveled. They used as transportation any moving thing that passed within reach. Each seed pod, the size of a large bean and the shape of a tiny football, was covered with barbs. But a cuckleburr, again proving it could scheme and plan, didn't just grow simple barbs. Each was sharp and hooked on the end so that it didn't just stick, it took hold and *clung*.

I have heard, and believe it is true, that it was a cuckleburr that inspired the invention of Velcro.

Now, exactly what that has to do with the people of Cuckleburr, I can't tell you unless it's that some of them were sharp and tough and determined and, if they seized upon something or some idea, they never let go.

But, back to the school: we had two possible routes to get there, one about a mile and the other about two and a half miles long. The shortest route led down the dredge ditch from our house, followed it through a stretch of woods, and then took a country lane on the other side that came out near the school. If we chose to do so we could use the longer route which we called "going around the road." That way we walked the mile out to the Broadmoor store, turned south for a mile down the paved Highway 78 and turned left onto a gravel road to the school.

We enjoyed the walk through the woods as it engendered a feeling of closeness with nature but, that way, there was no one to walk with us. If we went around the road there would be other kids walking the same way and we enjoyed that more. Of course, when the weather turned nasty and cold, we took the most direct route.

Before the beginning of school each year, to make our walk through the woods easier, Daddy, using a scythe, cleared us a well-marked path. One winter was unusually cold and the dredge ditch froze over solidly enough that we could skate on it. Of course, we didn't have real skates but we could get a running start and then slide for a thrilling distance. As long as the ice held, we used that route every day.

The school building had two main rooms and a smaller room called the cloak room. The two rooms were divided by doors that could be folded back on themselves and pushed aside, creating one large room. At the end of one of the rooms was an elevated stage that, a few times a year, we used to put on improvised plays or programs. Students were divided according to grade, the first four grades in one room and the fifth through eighth, in the other.

The school had no electricity and was lighted only by the large banks of windows on one side. Of course, there was no air conditioning. In summer, the temperature was kept bearable by opening all the windows. In winter, each of the two main rooms was heated by a large, pot-bellied, coal-fired stove. These provided three levels of comfort. Like Goldilocks, we found them to be either too hot, too cold or just right.

We had two grand ladies as teachers. Mrs. Mary Glidewell, the principal, taught the higher grades and Miss Mary Jane House was in charge of the younger ones.

The cloak room was used, of course, to store our outer clothing and lunches and it was used for one other function that was never far from our minds. That was where all the paddling took place. In those days teachers believed in, and enthusiastically practiced, corporal punishment. "Miss Mary" had had a lot of practice and was quite good at it. Few days passed without one of those other boys testing her.

I once had a picture, long since lost, taken by a professional photographer of the whole student body and I wish I could show it to you. There must have been at least twenty or twenty-five of us ranging in age and size from "Shorty" Gregory, who was about eighteen and six foot four, to the baby, Carol Strachn. I will tell you something about Carol in a moment.

When I remember Cuckleburr School, so many glimpses of my days there return to me and most, but not all of them, summon a smile or a laugh. I will tell you of a few of them.

I remember Ozell Hood. Once, when he and I were in the seventh or eighth grade, the teacher was supervising preparations to put on an evening's entertainment as we did from time to time. We knew the whole community would be there. So Ozell and I devised a skit of our own and petitioned the teacher to let us put it on without her seeing it first. She was reluctant to do that but, believing we were responsible boys, she finally relented. We could hardly wait for we thought it would be hilarious.

When, on opening night, the curtain rose on the newly-discovered act of Weaver and Hood, we were ready. We first told a few harmless jokes, me acting as straight man, and got a few chuckles. And then came our big one.

Ozell said to me he wanted to recite some poetry and I told him he didn't know anything about poetry. But he insisted and, at last, I told him to go ahead and he began:

"Roses are pink and violets are blue..."

I, of course, interrupted him and again pointed out he didn't know anything about poetry and that he had just proved it by saying roses are pink when everybody knows roses are red.

Well, we argued back and forth for a moment, building toward our punch line, and, when the timing was right, Ozell reached inside his shirt and pulled out a pair of underwear that belonged to his mama, a substantially built lady, whose name was Rosie.

Now, let me tell you, I'm not talking about wispy, dainty little panties; these were *drawers!*

Ozell, holding them high and stretching them to their full dimension for all to see, said, "Well, these are Rosie's and they are *pink!*"

That was quite risqué in that time and I am sure it shocked the ladies but it also brought the house down. They were rolling in the aisles, everybody, that is, but Rosie and the teacher who must have broken some sort of record in getting us off the stage, all the while threatening to kill us and apologizing to the audience at the same time!

It was while I was a student at Cuckleburr that I saw my first movie. The name and the subject of the movie now escape me but it was something the school system wanted every student to see. It was being shown in Dyersburg at the high school gym and a bus was sent out to carry us there and back. We sat on bleachers and groups of students from different schools were intermingled. When one showing was completed they just started over again. They never turned on the lights. When one group had seen the whole program they were supposed to get up and go out.

Well, I was so engrossed in the film that I didn't notice when the others from our school left without me. Then, when I finally did look around, I suddenly realized I was all alone in a crowd of people I didn't know. Boy, I was scared! I was near panic, fearing the bus had gone and left me and I didn't know how I would get home. I didn't even know which direction to start.

But I got a grip on myself and decided the best thing I could do was nothing; just stay where I was and hope somebody would come and get me. Finally, sure enough, one of the teachers did come for me. I never knew what I was supposed to learn from the movie but, that day, I did learn that a city can be a fearful thing, lying in wait to trap a poor, confused country boy.

This is Gene again.
Speaking of lessons learned, let me tell you of one:
I think of this as the day the bully whipped Johnny. I was probably about eleven or twelve the year Johnny came to our school. While I was then relatively small, I was fast on my feet and was fairly agile so that I usually acquitted myself well in the roughhouse-type games we boys played at recess. Being accustomed to competing with a group that included boys several years older than me, I had developed a degree of toughness. Though, in most games, I was usually bested by older and bigger boys, I held my own pretty well, up to a point.

But Johnny couldn't do that. Or he wouldn't. He was much larger and probably a couple of years older than me but he had entered school in my grade. For reasons unexplained, although he wasn't dull or mentally deficient, he had dropped behind in his studies. Though he had the physical attributes, he wasn't emotionally prepared to compete in contests involving physical strength. He just wouldn't dig in and use the strength he appeared to have.

I didn't admire Johnny but he, for reasons of his own, seemed to pick me as a friend. I was then somewhat academically advanced so that, when Johnny needed help with his reading or arithmetic, he would come to me. On the playground, too, he always seemed to be near. And, for reasons I didn't attempt to define, I resented his emotional weakness as if, by picking me as a friend, he was painting me with the same brush. Still, there was some advantage in having Johnny around. Here was someone I could dominate and could bully and bend to my will and that made me feel important.

I now realize that my attitude toward Johnny was evidence of an emotional problem of my own but I didn't recognize it at the time. Then the day came when emotional dominance wasn't enough. I had to make it physical.

That day, without reason, I suddenly turned on Johnny, who thought I was his friend, and, with all my strength, drove my fist into his belly. And then, just in case, I darted out of his reach, but I soon saw that move was unnecessary.

As I watched, Johnny; big, strong but emotionally weak Johnny, simply seemed to melt before me. With both hands he clutched at his abdomen, struggling to recover the breath my blow had knocked out of him, and I began to have second thoughts about what my one-blow victory might have proved.

Then I looked into his face and what I saw there became a lesson I have carried with me throughout my life. The first thing I saw was surprise, and then disbelief, and then disappointment and pain, and, at last, acceptance; acceptance of the truth that there are those in this world who will take from you all you give—your admiration and your loyalty and your friendship—and then will betray you and discard as worthless all the things you value most.

I have always had a hope that, somewhere down the road, Johnny found a friend better than me who taught him what true friendship is.

But, of the two of us, I think I learned the greater lesson. I learned that, in attaining dominance over one who has not the will to resist, there is no victory for the bully.

After that day, I tried to treat Johnny better but I am ashamed to say I didn't have the decency or the guts to tell him outright that I was sorry or to thank him for teaching me, the bully, perhaps the most important lesson of my life.

Now, this is Bueford again:
I have so many memories of my days at Cuckleburr School but I won't attempt to tell you all of them, but I remember.

There was Droopy Pierce. (We gave him that nick name.) His family moved down from some city in Illinois. They were much more sophisticated and affluent than the rest of us but that didn't lead Droopy to assume an air of superiority. Instead, it led to embarrassment for him. None of us local kids had special school clothes. We wore to school the same overalls we wore in the fields and, in the warm months, we sometimes came barefooted. Droopy's mother made him wear knickers, socks and shoes. We laughed at his clothes because they looked strange to us and we called the knickers "droopy drawers" and that led to the nick name. Though we instinctively liked and accepted him, we ragged him unmercifully for being different. But Droopy took it all in good humor.

Fortunately for him, his mother finally understood and allowed him to discard the offending garments and, thereafter, let him wear real clothes. But, in our minds and memory, no matter how he is dressed, he will always be our friend, Droopy.

I remember Joe Heathcott. At Cuckleburr we had no organized sports program but would often choose up sides and play baseball, that is, if we could scrounge up a ball and a bat. Between us, we had a few gloves but one thing we didn't have was equipment for a catcher. The only one who had the nerve to get behind the plate without mask or pads, and without even a catcher's mitt, was Joe so he would always catch for both teams.

One day, with Joe blocking the plate, one of the boys was trying to score on a close play. As Joe stood in there, waiting for the throw, the other boy ran him down and Joe came out of the incident with a broken nose. But, blood and dirt and all, Joe came up grinning.

After that, his dad somehow found the funds to buy Joe a real catcher's mitt and mask. Do you think the rest of us were envious? Absolutely not. Joe was our catcher and we thought of his new equipment as *our* mitt and *our* mask and we were as proud as he was.

And, of course, I remember Vernon. I remember my brother, Vernon. Vernon was born with an innocent charm glowing out of his eyes that no one could resist. Everybody liked Vernon and trusted him instinctively. In early school years he was classified as a slow learner but he wasn't. In fact, he may have had more native intelligence than any of us, but he was practical. The way he saw it, if he could skate through without unnecessarily taxing his brain, why not? He even seemed to enjoy the recognition his classification afforded him.

Throughout his life, Vernon found doors open to him that were firmly locked and barred for others. In adulthood, he changed jobs often and we have seen him, time after time, walk into a plant, past an emphatic, "Not Hiring" sign, and come out with a job.

In school there was a year that they were having some sort of parade in Dyersburg and all the county schools were invited to enter a float. Our school accepted the invitation. Our float wasn't very elaborate; just a borrowed field trailer pulled by half a dozen kids, and with some bunting attached, and with a royal couple, a King and Queen and their court, riding on it.

Who do you think sat up there, proud and tall, as The King? Right! It was Vernon. And you could see in his eyes the confident knowledge that here was where he was meant to be, riding somewhere above all worry or care, with his pretty queen, Evelyn Welch, by his side, while we commoners down below pulled the load. Of course, I was one of the humble mules pulling the wheeled throne. But I was proud of my brother.

There were many others I remember from Cuckleburr: Glenn Boswell and his brothers and sisters; John and Martin Ayers, Ralph Sanford, the Lay kids, and many more. And, of course, I remember the baby, Carol Strachn.

I promised, earlier, to tell you something about Carol but I have saved that story until the last for it is difficult for me to tell. Carol was tiny and, at that time, I thought, the prettiest little thing I had ever seen. The teachers sometimes assigned some of us older ones to help the young ones and I was assigned to help Carol and she was a joy to me.

Then one day, suddenly and irrevocably, she was gone.

Carol's family lived near Highway 78. That day, without looking, she started out to cross the road and ran into the path of a pickup truck and was killed instantly. I was stunned. It was the first time I had to deal with death and it broke my heart. And it brought questions to my mind that, though I knew they weren't logical, begged, nevertheless, for answers. Why did death have to be so swift and so permanent? Surely, God could give us a few more moments; a chance to see her alive again; to say to her I knew not what, but *something*.

Of course, I knew what the answers were. Carol was just dead; she was gone.

In that time, it was the custom, not to leave them at the funeral home, but to bring the dead back home to lie in state until burial and I wanted so bad to go and see Carol. But Mama told me I shouldn't. I had outgrown and outworn my shoes from the previous year and didn't have anything suitable to wear. I would have had to go barefoot. Mama told me that just wouldn't have been right. So I didn't go to see her.

It's been more than sixty years, now, since that time but my memory of it is still fresh. In the ensuing years I have known death to come to many, including one of my own children, and I have found a faith that tells me everything has a purpose. Although I do not fully understand His purpose in everything, I trust Him. And we who trust Him do not walk life's pathway alone. I find joy and peace in His company, even in the most difficult times of life. One day I will end this earthly journey and walk home with Him and he will make all things clear.

19

Daddy Was a Beekeeper

Of all the characters I have mentioned, or will mention, in this book, the one who had the most profound influence on my life, and the lives of my brothers, is my daddy. In the first place, he was different from the others in the way he earned his livelihood. He was never a farmer. He was a beekeeper. There were brief periods that he did other things but, in his heart, he was always a beekeeper.

I have known others who claimed to be beekeepers that did little more than harvest the honey when the hives became full. The bees did all the work. But not Daddy. He cared for his bees. It was almost as if he and they had an agreement: Daddy would take care of them and they would take care of him. I am convinced that, on some level, there was communication between them.

When at last I reach my eternal reward, and, if I find myself in a land of milk and honey, I will fully expect to find the one tending the hives is my own daddy.

He *believed* in bees and believed the honey they produced could do more for our health than any other one thing on earth. He avowed that a bee sting was the best thing one could do for arthritis and, when he was troubled with it, he would catch a bee and coax a sting from it.

In our part of the country, Daddy was well known and respected in the beekeeping industry. Done right, keeping bees was hard work, but not to Daddy. His attitude toward his bees brings to mind the picture of the orphan boy who, one dusky evening, appeared at the gates of Boys Town carrying another on his back. When someone suggested he must be tired, he replied "He ain't heavy, Father. He's m'brother." Daddy did, in fact, sometimes carry his bees on his back, moving them to locations with better access to the nectar from which the honey was made. They weren't, exactly, his brothers but they were close kin.

Daddy was disappointed when I didn't join him in his business and become a beekeeper like him. I helped him some in cleaning and repairing equipment and in preparing the harvested honey for market. But I had one disqualifying characteristic: I didn't like getting stung. Bees, for the most part, are not naturally vicious and will normally sting only under provocation. I told myself that repeatedly but, when they were buzzing around me, I forgot that part and was too nervous to concentrate on my work.

I did help Daddy when he took his honey to market. Daddy wholesaled some of it to grocery stores, but sold most of it directly to individuals. In the days prior to WW II, most southern towns had a street where persons with any kind of produce to sell could set up and offer it to the passing public. Most country folk, while in town, would wander through the market street and would often buy.

From the time I was about nine years old, I would go with him on these trips. Daddy would take the back seat out of his car and pack it full of honey we had packaged for sale and, when we arrived at the town targeted for the day, we would find a parking place and set up a display of our wares on a little table. Then we would wait for the customers.

Many potential buyers wanted a taste of the honey before they would buy. To accommodate them, we kept an open container and a kitchen knife with which they could dip out a taste and savor it. I'm sure the health department or the FDA or somebody would prohibit that practice today but, in those days, people weren't so picky.

Some of the people, after tasting the honey, would argue that it had sugar or something mixed with it but then, satisfied they had established themselves as a wise and discriminating shopper, they would buy it anyway.

After he gained the confidence that I knew how to count money and make change, Daddy would leave me for a while and go about other things. But he would come back now and then and pick up most of the money for fear someone might try to rob me or trick me out of it. Now and then someone would try to confuse me and cheat me on the change but they would fail. They couldn't fool me. When Daddy returned, some of these would laugh and tell him how they had tried but had been unable to beat me.

Two of our best markets were Jackson and Bemis, Tennessee. When we went there we usually stayed three or four days. At Bemis there was a big cotton mill and the management would let us set up near where the employees exited the plant. We would only do this for one afternoon for anybody who was in the market for honey would likely buy then. We would spend the rest of the time in Jackson.

I liked going to Jackson for, there, we would stay with Grandpa Weaver's sister and her husband, Aunt Sarilda and Uncle A. D., where we slept in a bed on a screened back porch and I enjoyed that, sleeping out in the fresh air.

Aside from paying for essential expenses, Daddy always paid me well for my help on these trips. On the last day there he would give me a dime. And I always spent it in the same way. There was a dime store there that sold a particular kind of ball for ten cents. It looked like a real baseball and was of the proper size and weight but it didn't have a leather cover. To form a cover, it was apparently dipped in some rubber-like material. When put into play and struck by the bat, the cover of the ball would soon begin to split but, until then, it worked fine. Always, when the other boys of Broadmoor knew I was going on a trip to Jackson, they would all urge me, "Don't forget the ball!"

We always did well in Bemis and Jackson and would come back with a pretty good bankroll. Once, we got a scare. We thought we were going to get robbed. Way out in the middle of nowhere a woman hitch-hiker was standing beside the road and Daddy stopped to give her a ride. When she approached the open window she asked innocently, "Can my little brother ride too?" Of course, Daddy agreed. Then, from out of the bushes there cane a huge, fully-grown man and it was too late for us to drive away. The man and woman got in the back seat and we drove on, but fearfully.

We were scared but I guess we misjudged them for we finally reached a place they wanted off. We escaped robbery that time but that was the last time we ever stopped for a hitch-hiker.

20

The Store

Except for the fields where we worked, and the churches, and the woods and paths and ditch banks where we children played, there was only one gathering place on Broadmoor. That was the store; not a general store, not a grocery store, not a hardware store, just The Store. For most of the time we lived there, it was run by Waltie Kennedy. Waltie lived on the premises with his wife, Hester, and his two girls, Metha and Sue.

The store occupied the ground level of a two-story building. Upstairs, arranged shotgun fashion, were the three rooms where Waltie and his family lived. Their access was by way of an outside stairway up the south wall of the building that ended on a small landing from which a door opened into the kitchen. On the front there was a porch, or maybe it should properly be called a gallery, above the lower level porch and store entry. There was no plumbing and, until around 1945 when the first power line came through, no electricity. Water had to be pumped out of the ground by hand and carried upstairs in a bucket. On a back corner of the lot there was an outhouse that not only served the family but was also used as a public facility by anyone else who felt the need.

The store was located downstairs in the one main room and one smaller room in back. Near the front of the larger room was an area that served as a kind of informal men's club in times when there was no farm work to be done. (Calling it a club might be elevating it a notch or two above what it deserved but it was a place to gather and socialize.) Women and girls came to the store to shop but they usually did their business and left, leaving the socializing to the men. (Chauvinism had not yet been identified as the evil it later became.) Weather permitting, we younger boys usually found things to do outside and so, we also, left the men to themselves. But when we were forced inside by the elements we squeez in to sit and listen to the gossip and tales and lies of our elders.

In the social area there were rough benches along two walls that provided seating for eight or ten adults and, when more were in attendance, they found a coke case or some kind of crate to sit or lean on. In winter a pot-bellied stove sat in the center of this area. A service counter ran along one side of the room. Behind it and all the way down that wall, and down the back half of the other wall, were shelves and cases holding merchandise. Up front there was a glass-front candy case, a cooler for "cole-dranks" and, later on, a freezer to hold ice cream and other frozen treats.

The small back room held bulk items, such as twenty-five or fifty pound sacks of flour, stands of lard, sacks of cornmeal and beans and the coal oil barrel.

Out front was a gas pump with a calibrated see-through tank. When an automobile stopped for gas Waltie would pump the amount ordered up from the supply tank in the ground into the calibrated tank and then let it drain through a hose and nozzle into the vehicle's tank. To prevent unauthorized dispensing of gas (I mean stealing) the pump handle was removed and locked up inside the store at night. However, this precaution was not one hundred percent effective. It was still possible, by substituting a monkey wrench or some similar tool for the handle, to pump up the gas. I think transient people did that from time to time but I doubt that any of the locals were that dishonest.

The men and boys who gathered in the social area were, for the most part, not there as store customers and they seldom bought anything, except, now and then, one might wander over to the cooler and get him something cold to drink. Nobody drank a soda or a pop or a cola. It was always either a "cole-drank" or a "coke." Most people called any kind of a soft drink a coke, as in, "What kind of a coke you want—a Orange Crush? a RC? a Pepsi?"

Sometimes a big spender might offer a drink to one or more of his buddies and, on rare occasions, might set 'em up for the house but that could be expensive. I remember once, during WW II, when Hub Henderson, home on leave with a pocket full of army money, set 'em up for the house and, at a nickel a drink, had to lay down some thirty-five or forty cents. Cash money. I remember that because I was one of the drinkers he treated. I had a Grapette.

The store was owned by Mr. Dunlap who also owned and operated a larger store in Ridgely and he hired a live-in manager for the Broadmoor store. When we first moved to Broadmoor the manager was W. B. Simpson. Waltie became manager when Dub-Bee left about 1939 and he stayed until the store closed in December, 1955.

Even on Sundays, when the store was closed, except in inclement weather, the store was the gathering place for the local male population. Weather permitting, we sat and lounged around on the front porch. In winter, on bright Sunday afternoons, we would gather on the south side of the building where we were sheltered from the north wind and warmed by the sun.

I was very young when we first moved to Broadmoor but, as I grew older, I began, like every other member of the male population, to hang around the store during idle times. I don't recall that I even thought about it then but I now see that Waltie and his family, while they didn't complain, were permitted no real privacy except when they were inside their living quarters upstairs. We loiterers treated everything but the living quarters as public property.

We were, however, always careful not to be rude or discourteous to the family and we expressed no resentment at the inconvenience suffered when some of us had to get up or move aside to allow Hester or the girls to thread their way through the crowd. Nor were they rude to us; always being polite and saying "Excuse me" as they passed.

But looking back, now, I wonder why Waltie and Hester didn't sometimes lose patience and come out swinging, she with a broom and he with a ball bat, and sweep us aside like the riff-raff we were.

21

Membership and Games

The group that gathered at the store on Sunday afternoons was not the same as at other times. Mostly, on the Sabbath, the senior males of the community stayed home, leaving the twenty-ish and thirty-ish men, and those of us boys that were not off roaming the woods, to carry on without them.

There was a great deal of talk among the men and a great deal of listening on the part of the boys. The talk was often bawdy and laced with scatology and references to inter-gender relationships to which we younger ones listened with eager interest. (Tellers of these stories only spoke in general terms, never referring to wives or girlfriends or any other specific person.) No effort was made to shield tender ears that might be present. With no expectation that grown men would lie about, or misrepresent, such things, we listeners acquired a great deal of knowledge in the matter of male/female relations, only later to learn at the hands of more tender and caring instructors that we had, in many ways, been misinformed.

I expect it will be difficult, probably impossible, for one born and raised in this modern age to appreciate the depth of the boredom that over-powered and weighed us down in the years and society that I speak of. There was, quite literally, nothing to do. Television hadn't been invented. Most families on Broadmoor couldn't afford radios. There were no telephones to call up and chat with a friend or one's mama. There were too many kids and too little privacy for love in the afternoon. Hunters among us could not take the field since hunting on the Sabbath was a sin. No one could afford to go out to a movie where a ticket cost as much as a quarter with popcorn another nickel on top of that. For the rare man who had access to a car, the cost of gas for a Sunday drive was prohibitive. There was, like I said, nothing to do.

So how did one fill the hours? At Broadmoor, he went out to the store where he joined the others who squatted and hunkered there in the sun and he whittled and he spit and he either told or laughed at old jokes and lied about women. And sometimes he played games; anything to dispel the all-encompassing boredom.

One very exciting game was pitching washers. The only equipment required was six washers, preferably about the size and weight of a silver dollar. The playing field was prepared by scratching three in-line holes in the dirt, the holes separated by about a foot. Then three other holes were dug in a similar manner about eighteen to twenty feet distant from the first. Then two players, each with three washers, would stand by one set of holes and pitch at the other, the object being to pitch your washers so that they fell or slid into one of the holes. The players would then walk to the other end, total their points, and pitch the washers back to the other set of holes. Each of the three holes had a different value. I forget the point count and the number required to win but, of course, the player that acquired the most points won. It could be competitive and fun for the players but it wasn't easy to get the crowd involved in the game.

One of the games played by the men that I now, in retrospect, find most amusing was marbles. Yes, I said marbles. There was one year that, for reasons that probably no one ever really knew, the men—grown, twenty- and thirty-year-old men—got to shooting marbles! I guess, if you stop and think about it, them shooting marbles is no more ridiculous than pitching washers or horse shoes or playing mama-peg, but it's a game so associated with children that just the thought of men playing it brings a smile. But, boy! Did them men have a time! Swapping taws and trading glassies and shouting "You fudged!" and "Hard-down knucks!" and "No roundance!" and "Liners are out!" and carrying on like they were a bunch of eight-year-olds and, all the while, having themselves a regular ball and not one bit embarrassed by it all.

Come to think of it, maybe the world would be a better place today if we could get our modern world leaders to come down off their high perches and shoot a little marbles; get them to swapping taws and trading steelies and glassies rather than counting their nuclear arms.

I mentioned mama-peg. That's what we called it but I think the real name is mumble-peg, or maybe mumblety-peg. Anyway, for you who never played it, it's a one-time popular game played, mostly, by young boys. I'm sure it's not played at all in these times for the principal equipment for a game is a pocket knife. Today, a kid can wind up in jail, or, as a minimum, expelled from school for possession of a pocket knife. But, in my youth, any country boy that could afford it owned one.

To play mama-peg, you must have a knife with at least two blades. You open fully the shorter blade so that it extends straight from the handle. Then, you open the longer blade half way so that it extends downward at a ninety-degree angle from the first. The playing board is a wooden bench or a length of plank. The player, holding the knife, lightly taps it so that the point of the ninety-degree blade sinks slightly into the wood, just enough that the knife can stand alone. Then, holding a finger under the handle, with a quick flick of the wrist, the knife is flipped up into the air. The object is to have it come down and land with one blade, or some combination, sticking in the wood so that the knife stands. Points are scored accordingly. If it does not stand at all, there are no points. If it lands and remains standing on only the shorter blade, with no other part touching down, the player gets one hundred points. If it stands alone on the ninety-degree blade, the score is seventy-five. Landing and standing with both blades touching down yields fifty points and, finally, if the knife lands and stands with the ninety-degree blade and the back end of the knife handle touching down, the point count is twenty-five. I forget what total is required to be declared a winner. Again, as a spectator sport, like pitching washers, mama-peg was only about one step up from whittlin' and spittin'

Let me tell you of one other game we played; one with a little more action, and one requiring some degree of athletic skill and, on the part of us younger ones, at least, some considerable nerve. This was a sort of combination of the track and field athlete's hop, skip and jump; the gymnast's vaulting horse, and the child's game of leap frog. We called it One-and-Over. Like all our games, it was simple in concept. Any age could and did play it, from adults all the way down to smaller boys. Here's how the game was played.

First, by some orderly means, two people were selected, one to be the down-man and the other the leader. The leader would select a base line and mark it by drawing his toe across the ground. The down-man would take his position by standing at the base line and bending over and gripping his ankles with both hands. As many others as wanted to play would line up and, one by one, would vault over the down-man's back, being allowed to touch his back with their hands and support their weight as they passed over. The last in line was the leader.

As the leader landed beyond the down-man, he would drag a toe laterally in the dirt to mark a new spot and the down-man would move up and take his new position and the leader would call the play; either "Over" or "One-and-over." The other participants would again line up and, using the original base line as their starting point, would again vault, or attempt to vault, over the down-man without knocking him off his stance.

If the leader's call was Over, they were required to take off from the base line and, without touching the ground between, clear the down-man. They could, and usually did, back off and get a running start. If the leader's call was One and Over, they could touch the ground once between the base line and the down-man's back. Any participant who failed to complete the vault without displacing the down-man was out of the game.

Again, the leader would be last in line and he, also, had to complete the vault as he had called it. If he successfully completed the vault he would, upon landing, drag his foot establishing yet a new position for the down man and, again, would call it: One and Over, Two and Over, etc., according to his estimate of the number of hops or touch-downs he believed he would require to complete the vault.

If the leader failed to complete any vault as he had called it, he was out and the next in line moved up to leader. Any other player who failed to successfully complete the vault as called was out of the game.

The game would continue in this way until only one was left and he was declared the winner.

This might not sound like much of a game but, after the first two or three rounds when the call stretched out to multiple "and overs" it could begin to get interesting and the pressure would begin to build, particularly on the down man, and more especially if he happened to be one of the smaller boys. Picture yourself, a seventy-five or eighty pound kid, bent over from the waist, clutching your ankles and looking through your legs as some full-grown man, two or three times your weight, comes huffing and charging up to the base line and launches himself at you and you've got to stand there knowing the odds are he will hit you like a load of bricks and knock you sprawling. That took a little bit of nerve. And it produced a great many spills and laughs.

I don't recall anyone ever being hurt beyond a few bruises and scratches but we did have some pretty interesting collisions from time to time. I think One and Over may never be advanced to an Olympic sport but maybe the committee should consider it. It can offer action and spills, test athletic prowess and determination, generate laughs and maybe a little blood and it would be at least as interesting as soccer.

22

Other Kids, Other Scenes

Everybody on Broadmoor, including us kids, all seemed to get along and serious disagreements or conflicts seldom developed. Actual fights were rare indeed. But there were exceptions. I remember the day Billy Eaton turned pro.

Billy and some other kid (I don't even recall which it was) were snarling at each other and outright fisticuffs became a possibility. Actually, I doubt that either of them wanted that but they found themselves, with no blows having been struck, but faced off, toe to toe, their fists doubled up and faces wrinkled in anger, each, I think, hoping the other would back down.

But several of the adults standing by saw the chance of generating some action to stir a little dust. They were laughing and egging the would-be combatants on; especially K. P. Lay. Of course, this was all in fun on the adults' part. They knew, whatever happened, no one was going to get injured.

Anyway, K. P. saw it as his duty to get things moving and so, when nothing seemed to be happening, he pulled out a whole nickel and offered it to Billy if he would hit the other boy. Now, as I said, Billy wasn't all that anxious to fight but here was a chance, not only to establish himself as a pugilist but, in his first appearance for pay, to claim the entire purse for himself, win or lose.

Well, we onlookers could see the wheels turning in Billy's mind and saw he was weighing possible profit against potential loss. At last, the money became too much for him. He told K. P. to hold out his hand with the nickel laying in it. Then, when he had psyched himself up sufficiently, he snatched the nickel with one hand, and simultaneously landed a light blow on the other boy with the other and took off running at top speed. As far as he was concerned, he had landed the only blow and had been paid for his effort, and, thus, had won and the bout was over. And he was right. The other boy was by then laughing so hard any pursuit of the fleeing Billy would have been futile.

It was a one-punch fight, reminiscent of Louis and Galento, but I think K. P. got his nickel's worth just the same and it's provided me many a nostalgic laugh over the years.

I recall another boy who, one time, like Billy, came face to face with the temptation of sudden riches; a lure too strong to deny. Only, his temptation was not cash money. It was much more valuable than that. It was a fortune in candy. I will refrain from naming the boy but will tell his story.

It wasn't right, really, for one so young to be confronted daily with the presence, just beyond the glass face of the candy case, of untold wealth in the form of gum drops and Milky Ways and Double Bubble and peppermint sticks and all manner of other confections. For one who very seldom had even a penny to spend, it was too much. So he made a plan.

One evening, near the store's closing time, the boy surreptitiously stole into the back storage room, found a hiding place and allowed himself to be locked in, along with his sweet tooth and all that candy. It was his plan to eat his fill and then let himself out the front door and nobody would be the wiser.

But there were two major flaws in his plan. First, he found his eyes were bigger than his stomach and he was soon filled up to here. Then, when he tried to let himself out, he found the door was secured by a key-operated deadbolt and, of course, Waltie carried the key on his belt. He was caught like a mouse in a trap; a well-filled mouse, but a trapped mouse nevertheless.

He could only wait and plan his story until, when he didn't come home for supper, his anxious parents would come looking for him. When, at last, he heard their cries, he responded and they got Waltie to spring him loose. He came up with a perfectly believable story; that he had fallen asleep in the storage room on a sack of chickenfeed and it was dark when he awoke. They might have believed him except for all the empty candy wrappers they found laying around. We hope that ended the boy's criminal career.

One of my friends in the early years at Broadmoor was a boy named Shirley, Shirley McDaniel. He was exactly my age, both of us sharing the birthday of July 26, 1927. In later years, I learned that most people with that name were girls but we had no doubts about Shirley's masculinity. He was very athletic and, in our boyhood group, was always an organizer and a leader. We each often visited in the home of the other.

Shirley's dad was a lot of fun. He drank a lot and was, much of the time, somewhat under the influence but he was never mean or abusive. Mr. Mac

(That's what everybody called him.) had a flatbed ton and a half truck and he made his living hauling stuff in it. As far as I know, that was all he did. When he was home and Shirley's mother was not (She was Miz Mac.), he liked to get some of us boys on the truck and drive around the yard. We enjoyed that immensely. Except for the day he ran under a clothesline that none of us had seen and swept us all off. As far as I know, that was as close as any of us ever came to getting hung.

But I once had another, and very serious, brush with the man with the scythe and I believe, that day, Shirley saved my life. In a book he wrote a few years ago, called *Mama Never Cried,* my brother, Larry Weaver (We call him by his middle name, Gene) wrote about that day. This is what he wrote.

> Some three or four miles from where we lived on Broadmoor was a major drainage ditch, locally called Bee-Varm ditch. As far as I know the origin of the name was lost in the past, but it might have been a contraction for "Beaver Arm." I don't know.
>
> Anyway, during most of the year it was a slow, murky stream, maybe twenty to twenty-five feet across, meandering lazily on its way that would lead it into other streams and, eventually, into the Mississippi. But when the spring floods came it grew into a surging, muddy river doing its job of moving the overflow and, at the same time, throwing out a challenge to youthful and daring swimmers.
>
> One spring, when I was about ten or eleven, I tagged along with a group of older boys, Bueford and Vernon included, who walked up to Bee-Varm to see the flood. Most of the older boys were fairly good swimmers, and, of course, the question of swimming the ditch arose. I think they had known all along that they would take the dare.
>
> They decided to go and to cross as a group. Throwing off every stitch, they plunged into the raging stream. One who made the trip was Shirley, of about the same age as Bueford, then probably fourteen or fifteen. Shirley was strong, athletic, and a leader.
>
> They made it across without incident and rested a while and, since all their clothes were on the other side, had no choice but to re-cross. It was then that Mama came as close as she ever would to realizing her worst fear, the loss of one of her boys.
>
> The group entered the water slowly, still close together, and set out for the other bank, using a conservative stroke somewhere between a breaststroke and dog paddle. Nothing untoward happened until about mid-stream when Bueford suddenly cried out with the pain of a cramp and sank beneath the muddy waves. The moment the water closed over him he was lost from view in the ditch that was then probably fifteen or more feet deep. Willows that grew along the low-water banks were now thrusting out of the flood and, against

them, driftwood and other floating objects had collected. It was clear that if the current carried Bueford in among the trees, and if he could not effect his own escape, he would be gone.

Anything short of swift and decisive action would have been too little and too late. The only sense by which the others might find Bueford was that of touch; if they couldn't feel him, they couldn't find him, and if they couldn't find him he was lost.

With Shirley taking the lead, he and Vernon and the other swimmers also disappeared beneath the torrent, leaving me and one or two other younger boys to stand on the bank and watch and tremble.

Then, at last, almost as if by miracle and after what seemed an eternity, Vernon and Shirley broke the surface, towing Bueford between them as they struggled to the bank. The reaper had tried, but youthful strength and determination had won that day.

Later, as we were walking home, someone asked Bueford what it was like under the water. He said it was strange. He said that after the initial panic, when the darkness closed in and his mind told him he was about to die, a calmness came over him, and his thoughts were of Mama and then of Vernon, and he thought, "I'd rather be me than be him and have to go home and tell her."

We decided not to tell Mama about it at the time. As far as we know, no one ever did.

Of course, I didn't see any of this but I believe Gene was a reliable witness. I do know that when I regained consciousness, Shirley was giving me artificial respiration.

Without doubt, someone saved my life that day and I have always believed it was Shirley. But maybe, if he hadn't been there, someone else would have. Who is to say? Gene saw Vernon go down with Shirley and stay down and neither came back up until they could bring me with them. And it was the two of them together who dragged me to safety. I guess it doesn't matter which, if either, of them deserves the greater credit. But one thing I do know, I will remember what they did until my dying day.

23

Mister Sam and Them

When I first saw Mister Sam he was the manager of Broadmoor Farms and I was just a kid. His full name was Sam Fussell but to everybody on Broadmoor he was just Mister Sam. Most of them worked for him. This is a man you should know for he, probably more than any one, shaped Broadmoor. I will try to introduce you to him and I will begin by saying, without reservation, that Mister Sam was one of the kindest, most honorable men I ever knew.

There was humor in him. You could see it in his eyes and he could be easily brought to laughter. He was even tempered. Never did I see him provoked to anger; never heard him raise his voice to anyone. In managing the farm, he carried a heavy responsibility but he bore its weight easily and he felt no need to continually prove his authority. Those who worked for him accepted his leadership without question. They universally liked him and looked up to him. But, there was one who not only admired him but loved him unconditionally. Her name was Pearl.

Miss Pearl, we called her, and. if anyone knew him, she did. She lived with him, through good times and bad, for fifty-seven years.

Some time after Mister Sam was gone, Miss Pearl felt moved to write down some history of their life together. These are some of the things she wrote:

> I was 15 and I met a wonderful man. That was February and we got married in September, 1922. His name was Sam J. Fussell. So the next year we started our family. (She names the children: Hazel, Calvin Ray, Melvina, Samuel J. and, lastly, Peggy.)
>
> She talks about the depression that began in 1929, saying: We had hard times. Everything was cheap but getting hold of money wasn't easy. That fall (1929) we moved to Halls to make a crop. (Halls is a small Tennessee town a few miles south of Dyersburg.) We didn't get anything out of our crop but the picking. Our rent came first. (What she means here is, after the rent was paid, there was nothing left but a little money for the picking.) The cotton picking was hard so I took Bud (Calvin Ray was called Bud) with me and we went

across the creek to pick. I made enough to buy our clothes. A pair of shoes, they were a dollar a pair. There were two sets of clothes around for the kids and a few things for me and Sam. When the clothes got dirty I'd wash them out on a rub board at night and have them ready for the next morning for Hazel and Bud. They were going to school.

Food was cheap but getting hold of the money to buy it was hard. We raised and canned what we could. We picked dried peas and beans and had our chickens for our eggs so the man (on whose place they lived), he planted a big turnip patch that fall. His name was Mr. Thurmond. On Friday evening late we picked the greens, me and Sam and him, by the bushel basket and, on Saturday, they would take it to Dyersburg and go to the stores and sell it and swap it for groceries.

Flour was 49 cents for a 24-pound sack and they got meal. Coffee, it was 25 cents a pound and lard, you got a pretty good size bucket for 50¢. Sugar, they sold it by the pound. It was 10¢ a pound. And he would get a pretty big piece of salt pork. That was to cook with our greens and peas and beans and potatoes which we growed at home. I don't know a time when we went hungry. We set down and enjoyed it.

Our neighbors would give us milk and butter.

Once I chopped cotton a whole day, they was paying 50¢ a day, and got paid in a broom. I needed a broom and they fed us our dinner too.

We moved to Broadmoor and things got better. The next year (1934) we had our last baby, a girl. Her name was Peggy.

Well they (the children) are all grown up now with children of their own and grandchildren. I'm getting old, 74, and without my husband. We had 57 years together. It's lonely without him. He passed away in 1979. Sometimes I don't know why I keep on but the Lord knows best.

I want to be put up there beside their Dad...

Well, Miss Pearl eventually got her wish. For some years now, she has been up there beside Mister Sam and we who aren't there yet hope they have found a place where the cotton is all picked and there is always a big piece of salt pork to season their greens.

But let me tell you some of my own impressions of Mister Sam and his family. Compared to others in the community, he was a learned man. In the time and place he lived when he was young, education was not much sought after and it was not easy to come by. Most country people, if they had any schooling at all, were limited to a few years of grammar school. Mister Sam once told me how he, as a young man, made up his mind to get some education. His dad was one of those who didn't see any need for it and wouldn't let him go to school but he still held the dream. Finally, when he was about sixteen or seventeen, he made arrangements to go and stay with Mr. Barlow Parker and work for him while he went to school. Mr. Parker was the patriarch of a large family that later lived on Broadmoor, many of whom worked for Mister Sam. He was determined and he stuck with it until he completed the twelfth grade. For that time and place, that made him an educated man.

By the time we moved to Broadmoor he was manager of more than two thousand acres of prime farm land. We would see him driving over the land in his Model-T Ford. One of the first things I remember about him is that he would always slow the car when passing by our house in case one of us kids was in the road. And he never went by without waving.

It's strange, sometimes, what one will remember about another. One of my lasting pictures of Mister Sam is the way he could make the simple act of imbibing a soft drink look so good. He would, from time to time, stop by the store, sweating from his work, and go to the cooler for a "sodie water." He would pull the cap of his selection and wipe the top on his sleeve and turn the bottle up and take long draughts and the burbling sound of the liquid gushing from the bottle and the little gurgle in his throat with each swallow all became a deliciously tempting image to a thirsty boy building fantasies about some future time that he might be rich enough to have a sodie water any time he felt like it.

But there was much more to Mister Sam than just an image. He knew the people of Broadmoor and cared about them. He knew their strengths, their shortcomings and faults, their idiosyncrasies and, I think, even their private dreams and desires.

And, like I said, he was kind. There came a time, in the later years we lived at Broadmoor, when us boys and Mama (We were alone then) were barely getting by and we had to seek out every opportunity to earn a few dollars. Mister Sam knew that and he understood the shame we felt at being the poorest family in the community. When he had work, he wouldn't wait for us to come begging but would make a point in coming to Mama, as if he was the one in need, and would say "Reckon them boys could help me? I have a job that I sure could use them on if they could."

These weren't made-up jobs. What he offered was real work and we sweat for our money like every one else. The only charity involved was in his giving the work to us rather than to someone less needy. But he let us keep our pride. And that proved, I think, that he hadn't forgotten where he came from nor that there can be different kinds of hunger associated with being poor.

Early on, Mister Sam traded his Model-T for a '36 Ford pick-up, but he still drove carefully, especially when passing our house, or others where he knew children might be playing. He was naturally a careful driver but, in taking it easy around our place, he was obeying specific orders. He had received his instructions and he always got a big laugh out of telling the story of how that happened.

One day, he said, as he approached our house, he found Royce, who was then no more than three, standing in the road and waving him down. When he stopped, Royce came over and, dead seriously, cautioned him. Pointing down the road, he said "My brother (he was speaking of Lynn) just left going to the store. You be careful and don't run over him!" Then, satisfied he had been properly instructed, Royce allowed him to go on his way.

As I have said, Mister Sam was an honest and honorable man but there were times when some felt he carried this thing too far. There was a day when three of my brothers, Vernon, Gene and Lynn, committed a minor infraction of the rules they thought caused harm to no one but then along came Mister Sam and his honor. It was a warm, sunny day and the lovely voices of nature, speaking louder than duty, tempted them to play hooky from school. They did and they spent a blissful day roaming the woods, climbing trees, picking blackberries, wading in the bayou and just generally being free. Then, in one careless moment, they were caught. Suddenly, from out of nowhere, there was Mister Sam in his pickup. He, or course, immediately discerned the truth and, while he didn't scold them, he did something eminently worse. As he passed by our house later in the day, he stopped and told Mama on them.

Well, Mama held certain firm beliefs. One was that school attendance was mandatory and another was that instruction will sometimes be better remembered if punctuated by corporal punishment. When the boys got home that day, Mama was laying for them and, through the vigorous application of the latter, she reminded them of the former.

And so what had been a lovely day came to a bad end, and it was Honor that did it, Honor and Mister Sam.

But Mister Sam also applied his code to his own children. He never whipped them. He left that to Miss Pearl, but he had his ways. When he set them down and gave them a good talking to I bet they would have preferred Miss Pearl and her switch.

There was a time when Bud got involved in what started out as a prank but ended up serious trouble. Some of the adult boys were always pulling pranks on each other. One Saturday night, up at Ridgely, several of them, including Bud, spotted a number of packages that some of the others had left in an unlocked car parked on the street and they thought how much fun it would be to take them and let the others think they had been stolen. Gleefully, they did so. Only thing was, it was the wrong car and the wrong packages and what started out as a prank ended up being treated as outright thievery. The culprits were quickly identified and the police were not amused. The boys ended up in jail.

Beginning early the next day, the boys' families came, one by one, to bail them out; all, that is, except Bud. All that long, lonely Sunday, he sat there, staring through the bars, filled with dread at the prospect of facing Mister Sam; yet, at the same time, hoping he would come. But he didn't. For the whole long day Bud sat and contemplated his sins until, at last, his Dad came. Bud had prepared himself for the lecture he knew was coming and he waited. And he waited. But Mister Sam never said a word. All the way home, he let Bud sit there and bleed under the lash of his silence. We think Bud got the point.

Fortunately, the boys' explanation was accepted and they all got off with a light fine for some sort of disorderly conduct charge.

Miss Pearl was a strong woman. She was small in stature but large in determination and spirit. One event, I think, kind of sums her up. It was cold and snowy and ice was on the ground and she had to be outside for some purpose and she slipped and fell and hurt her hip. It later turned out she had broke it. But she didn't tell anybody. She just got up, dusted the snow off, went back to the house, got her a broom handle for a walking stick and went on about her work. Others noted she limped some but she never complained or explained why. When anyone asked her about the limp she would say, "I'm doing all right. My old hip sort of bothers me sometime but it will be all right."

Ten years later she was persuaded to see a doctor and he scheduled her for hip replacement surgery. Afterwards, after he had seen the evidence, he asked her, "Mrs. Fussell, how in the world did you manage to walk on that hip all this time?"

Her reply was typical of Miss Pearl, "You do what you have to do. I had to take care of Sam."

Some would say she was stubborn but it was more than that. Stubborn has boundaries. Sprit is limitless. Miss Pearl was strong in spirit. That's how she lived, devoting her life to her God, Sam, and her family; not necessarily in that order.

If you need further evidence, I think you can read the character of Mister Sam and Miss Pearl in the children they raised. The oldest, Hazel, I never knew very well. She married and moved away early on and both she and her husband later died and were buried somewhere in Michigan.

The third child, the second girl, was Sis. Her real name was Melvina but I didn't know that for years. Everybody, including the family, just called her Sis. She was a lot of fun. You could see a hint of mischief shining out of her eyes but, as her later life proved, there was also strength there. When she was about seventeen, she left Broadmoor and found work in a cotton mill at Bemis, Tennessee. There, she met and married a man and they produced several of the nicest, kindest and most well-mannered children you would ever want to see. Apparently they inherited all these traits from Sis since their father never displayed any of them and she was left to struggle alone to bring the children up.

But she never complained about the hand life dealt her. There was one Christmas that my family and I learned Sis and her kids wouldn't be having any. It was a year that we had been blessed with more than we needed and we put together a gift of what we could and dropped it by. Knowing that such a donation sometimes embarrasses the recipient and produces a less than satisfactory reaction, I was somewhat apprehensive, But I needn't have worried. The gracious manner in which Sis accepted what we offered will always stand out in my memory as the classic proof of the universal truth that it is more blessed to give than receive.

The oldest boy, the second child, was Calvin Ray, the one called Bud. Bud was a couple of years older than I and we didn't pal around together but I watched him a lot around Broadmoor and learned from him and looked on him somewhat as my hero. He was smooth. Today, I guess we would call him cool. He could have been the model for the TV character, The Fonz. Not only did he wear a leather jacket like Fonzie, he was always "On" as we say in show biz. Any time Bud was in the group most eyes would be on him but he never gave any sign that he knew that.

One of the little one-act plays he put on for us could be called *The Egg and Him*. It would begin with Bud sitting quietly at the store among the usual gathering of story tellers and he would casually reach in his pocket and pull out the pocket knife he always carried and he would begin, slowly, to strop the blade on his boot. The talk would continue but eyes would begin to shift to Bud. After he was sure he had their attention, he would close and replace the knife and then, casually but deliberately, stand and walk over to the basket where Waltie kept the fresh eggs, and, still apparently unaware eyes were on him, he would make a great production of selecting the most suitable egg and would return to his seat. He would hold the egg in his hand for a while and roll it around and visually examine it as if trying to translate some ancient inscription on it and he would nonchalantly toss it in the air and catch it a few times.

As these parts of the drama played out, conversation would begin to fade. When he was satisfied the proper foundation had been laid, Bud would again reach for and open his razor-sharp knife. He would again hold up and examine the egg as if he were a surgeon deciding where to make the incision for a delicate operation. At last, satisfied, he would hold the egg up in one hand and, with the knife in the other, would slice off the top end of the shell, exposing the contents.

Then, still oblivious to the rapt attention of his audience, he would take the egg to his lips and, in one motion, toss down and swallow the contents and, when the room erupted with expressions of appreciation for his performance, Bud would modestly look about as if he had only just then become aware there were others in the room.

The fourth Fussell child was Samuel J, called Bo. Now, here was a character. He was about Vernon's age, a couple of years younger than me and, as we all grew up, we moved in much the same circles. That is, except for Bo's early years. When he was about six years old he was stricken with rheumatic fever and, for a long time, he was bedfast and, after that, his activities were curtailed for several years. He, thus, never had much opportunity to go to school. But Bo was, in many ways, in fact, in most ways, a genius. I never saw anything he couldn't do. I have often wondered what he might have accomplished had he had the benefit of a modern education.

While he was in bed, Mister Sam kept him supplied with things to keep his hands and mind busy, including clocks that Bo learned to take apart and reassemble. I'm sure that helped but Bo had an inborn ability to reason out any mechanical problem.

He became a master wood carver. He could pick up a piece of wood, envision some object concealed in it, a horse perhaps, and then, like the old joke says, he simply cut away anything that didn't look like a horse. Some of his best work was done in his later years when he became interested in carving miniatures.

He once set out to carve a replica of the Statue of Liberty in a single grain of rice and was near completion when he dropped it on a carpeted floor and could never find it.

Then he had an idea to carve a miniature violin. It was just something to do, he said, so he whittled out one slightly less than three inches long. Then he got serious. His next one was an inch and seven sixteenths and was made of black cherry tree bark. Thinking that might be some kind of a record, he checked with Guinness and found his fiddle was a whole half inch longer than the one listed as the world's smallest playable violin. When he read that, he said of the carver, "He's done got in my tree when it comes to whittling!" and he vowed to beat him.

As a first consideration, he researched and identified the most suitable kind of wood as the bark of the Osage orange tree. And, since there are no tools available for that kind of work, he made his own; knives from a sewing needle and one from a razor blade and he made a drill from a surgeon's needle and carved out a tiny vise to hold his work. And, of course, he used a microscope.

He fashioned eighteen separate pieces, glued them together and then strung the tiny instrument with almost invisible filament, one thousandths of an inch in diameter, used in eye surgery. He faced and overcame one of the greatest challenges when he made the tiny drill required to pierce the tuning keys to accept the strings.

When he was done he used a mixture of clear nail polish and paint thinner to varnish the tiny instrument and he constructed a carrying case about the size of a pea.

Bo, at last, had a violin that was thirteen thirty-seconds of an inch long, less than half the length of the Guinness record. But, alas, for some technicality, Guinness didn't accept it.

After he was finished, Bo and his fiddle was the subject of a feature article in The Memphis Commercial Appeal. It was a good article except for one thing. The reporter solicited comment from a music professor at Memphis State University who allegedly said of the violin, "Who plays it? A mouse or what? It may look like a violin but I doubt it plays like one." To which I say, well, Duh! Thank you, professor, for your brilliant and incisive reasoning!

I could tell you more stories about Bo, and probably will before I am finished, but, for now I will move on to other things.

But there is just one more thing before I leave the Fussells. In addition to all their other fine attributes, Mister Sam and Miss Pearl were generous. They gave freely of themselves to their friends and to the community but they saved their most valuable possession, their youngest daughter, Peggy; their pride and their joy, and they gave her to me. We were married June 6, 1952. Returning their generosity, Peggy and I eventually gave back to them seven fine grandchildren.

I may well have more to say about Peg later on.

24

The Boys

As we began to grow up on Broadmoor, we never wanted for friends and all of us got along well. There was plenty rivalry and competition in the games we played but very little argument or dissension and, except for Billy's Big Bout that I have spoken of, no fights at all. Over the years some moved away and some moved in; some outgrew us and some advanced from babyhood but a roll call of those who, at one time or another, were our Broadmoor friends would include: Shirley McDaniel; Carlton, Billy and Gaythal Eaton; The Johnson boys, Willard (called Hunt), Millard (called Fatty) and Leland (called Pee Wee) and their little brother, Bonnie; J.C and Gerald Buchanan; Junior Wolf and his younger brother, Johnny; Bud and Bo Fussell; Odie and Joe Parker and their uncle, Don; the Hendersons, Harvey and Joe; Oren Bissell; Melvin and Carmel Green; Buddy Green; and the Sellers boys, David (called Red) and Gene Autry; and there was William James, who was called Perchworthy.

Our circle of friends also included many from Cuckleburr, our neighboring community to the south, and from the school. I won't try to list them here but might refer to some of them later on.

There were, of course, a number of girls, and we counted them our friends, but they were not granted membership in our informal boys' club. After all, what would they know about climbin' trees and possum huntin' or spittin'? Most couldn't hit nothing with a slingshot and it would have been unseemly for them to come skinny dipping with us or join in a game of one-and-over.

When not at work or school, groups of us boys were always together and, if weather permitted us to be outside, were seldom still. We roamed the woods and the fields and often, when it was time to eat, would show up, en masse, at one house or another where they always managed to feed us. From where our house stood, Mama would usually see us coming when a group was about to descend on her at mealtime but she wouldn't panic. She always had a big pan of cornbread ready and she would just add a little more water to stretch the bean pot she kept simmering on the stove and she was ready for us.

It was likewise no problem when we brought two or three or four boys home with us to spend the night. In that time, as a matter of necessity, kids in most families slept several to a bed anyhow. So, when company came, what was a few more knees and elbows?

Mama always did her best to make our guests feel welcome and, mostly, I think, she genuinely enjoyed them but there was this one time. It was the Saturday before Easter and we were planning an egg hunt for the next day. A bunch of boys would be coming but Pee Wee and Fatty Johnson came early and spent the night and the spring weather was so warm and balmy that Pee Wee came barefooted. And when we got up on Easter morning there was a big snow on the ground! We were stuck in the house with Mama, or, I think it would be more accurate to say, she was stuck in the house with us! How she put up with us that live long day, I'll never know. That was an Easter I think none of us will forget.

Nights, and sometimes at other times, when weather kept us in, Mama would read to us. Some of the boys, I think, came as much to hear her read as to visit with us. One of those was Bo. His favorite stories were *Tom Sawyer* and *Huck Finn*. While Mama read, he would sit in rapt attention, eyes glowing and hanging on to every word. One of his favorite scenes was the one where Tom and Huck were sawing Jim out of his place of imprisonment and Tom insisted they dispose of the sawdust by eating it. It wouldn't be a proper adventure otherwise, Tom said.

Mama could make it all seem so real. Gene wrote some about that in his book about Mama and I quote him here:

> It was through her eyes that we first met Tom and Becky and Aunt Polly, and in her soft voice that we first heard the whisper of the river and the distant rumble of the steamboats as Huck and Jim drifted through the night, seeking a place to be free.
>
> Her reading brought life to Black Beauty and Lassie and Buck, the great lead-dog, and on cold nights, when the winds shook our little house and we children huddled safely around a warm stove, from the pages of a book she could summon the distant, lonely, haunting call of the wild.

I think Bo would have liked that.

Books were an important part of our life. We owned a few that we read over and over and, sometimes, though our school had no library, the teachers would go to the library in Dyersburg and bring back a selection we could borrow from.

Before I move on to other things, there is one more boy that I might have previously made some reference to but who I haven't placed in the story. He is my youngest brother, Royce. It was June 5, 1937, and we four older boys were at a cookout and sleep-in hosted by Bud and Bo. (Let me interrupt here. Bud did the cooking. I don't remember the main course, but one thing he cooked up was a big pan of fried potatoes. It was warm summertime weather and the lantern he used to see by was attracting a swarm of gnats. I remember that, when it came time to eat, the potatoes were covered with black flecks. In the poor light, we couldn't be sure if we were eating black pepper or fried gnats but, whatever it was, it was delicious.)

Bud had rigged a tarp as a tent and we planned to sleep under it on the ground. But, during the night, Daddy came and got us. He had a surprise for us. Mama had done her finest work and had produced our new brother. He was a little premature and had some early health problems but overcame them. However, he must have had some concerns that he had arrived in the right place when he looked up to see four sets of round eyes staring down at him and us pushing and shoving each other to get a better look.

Whatever he thought, we will never know for either he doesn't remember or he ain't talking.

I will briefly mention a couple more of the boys.

Junior Wolf was one of a kind. He was rowdy; he was fun; he entertained, and, very often, he led us into trouble. As he grew into his teens it became apparent that his life's ambition was to be known as the orneriest kid in the community. I think everyone who knew him would agree he not only reached that goal but exceeded it.

There is a story (a true one) he loved to tell. Once a local mother was complaining to Junior about how sorry one of her sons-in-law had turned out to be. As she recited a long list of the boy's sins, she grew more and more agitated until, at last, in final condemnation of the scoundrel, she said, "I tell you Junior Wolf, she wouldn't have been no worse off if she had married you!"

Junior would tell that story and practically roll in the dirt with mirth.

Don Parker was a good 'un. I'm not too proud of this story but I've got to tell it. Once, after we got old enough to buy beer, Don and I were up at Ridgely and had a couple too many and, having no transportation, we set out to walk back to Broadmoor. Don apparently thought I was in worse shape than him and, all the way, he lectured me to be careful and walk straight when we got to the store so no one would suspect we had been drinking and I assured him I could handle that. Then, when we arrived and stepped up on the porch, Don, the sober one, hung his toe and fell through the door, flat on his face in front of everybody! So no one suspected we had been drinking; they knew it for a fact!

In effort to dispel any notion you might have formed that all us boys were a sorry lot, I will give you a better example. All the Lays were hard workers and Purvis, just my age, was no exception. He was also a planner. One year, when we were still in grade school, his daddy let Purvis have an acre of land on which he could grow whatever he chose. Purvis grew corn, which might not have been the best cash crop, but he had a plan. He also bought a pig and he fed the corn to the pig. When she reached the age of consent, he introduced her to a boy pig and she produced a litter of piglets. When the little ones grew up and were marketed, rather than spending his money on some extravagance, Purvis salted it away until he could put it to good use.

That's how he started. By the time he was a young man, through such planning and wise investment, Purvis was tending thousands of acres and was known throughout the state for his farming and management practices.

25

More than Skin Deep

Thus far, I have pointedly avoided mention of one segment of the Broadmoor population and I suppose I have done that because I'm not sure how to handle it. I guess the only way to do it is tell the truth.

I am alluding to the Colored Folks. In my youth, that term was not thought to be derogatory. In fact, those who used it, rather than the more commonly used one, thought of themselves as being liberal. That was a time that, in the South, race was not a problem. We simply obeyed the rules. Of course, the whites made the rules and their rules were the only ones that mattered. Members of both races accepted that there was a line between them and the line was clearly drawn. In my youth, I never knew anyone to step over it.

A number of Broadmoor's citizens had skin of a darker hue. Their houses were all grouped together, separate from the whites, and they had their own church and school. White people not only felt that was right, but, if the subject ever came up for discussion, they all agreed that it was not only right (and supported by The Bible) but they would confidently declare the colored folks preferred it that way.

In the light of the present, it is plain we were then born and bred segregationists. Still, we found it easy to relate to the blacks without upsetting what we viewed as the natural order of things. We worked side by side for the same rate of pay and we young ones often played together. Special fun were the baseball games, we would get up, always Black against White. There was a very acceptable diamond out behind the Black church and school. We would meet there on Sunday afternoons and, by pooling our equipment, would gather a sufficient number of bats, balls and gloves for the game.

I will not tell you who usually won. I will only say that, on the ball field, we whites learned one truth. It was not in every endeavor that the blacks always sat in the back of the bus.

Not only did they beat us, they toyed with us. They had a very talented pitcher and I can still hear the catcher's encouraging words, "Throw it on in here, Ocie B. I know you swift enough!"

26

Floods and Things

Beside the birth of our new brother, nineteen thirty-seven was a year of adventure and change. Early in the year I was nine-going-on-ten, when things I didn't understand began to happen up-river, that is, in the northern reaches of the Mississippi. But I do remember we had rain, rain, rain. The drainage ditches and the Obion River and other streams began to overflow their banks and the water began slowly to creep toward our homes; ours, Grandpa's and Cheat and Aunt Reldie's. When our house became threatened, we moved in with Grandpa and Grandma, hoping we would be safe there but it soon became apparent we would all have to seek ground higher than that.

We, mostly the men, put what we could up above what we hoped would be the high water mark and assembled a few things needed for survival and prepared to flee to the hills, about four miles away. The adult men planned, once we were settled, to come back daily and check on the houses and what we were leaving behind but they would need a boat. I don't know where, but Daddy and Grandpa scrounged up the lumber and, though they had never taken on such a project before, they built a satisfactory boat.

While the rising water would still allow it, we loaded what we were taking with us into a wagon, hitched up a mule team and, with all of us aboard, turned east, leaving the flood behind. When I say all of us, I mean Mama, Daddy and all of us kids; Grandma and Grandpa, Dirk and Cheat and Aunt Reldie.

While we had made no specific arrangements, it was our plan to seek shelter, that first night, with folks we knew; maybe even stay a day or two, while looking for other quarters. These people were just a husband and wife and they lived in a comfortable home with plenty of room but, upon our arrival, they made it clear we were not welcome. I think that was the first time in my life that I felt humiliation; our being turned away by friends as if we were a band of roving Gypsies. We moved on and found a vacant house and made arrangements to use it and we stayed there until the flood receded and we could return home.

I don't remember how long that was but I think it was about a month. Our situation troubled the adults but we kids soon began to have fun. We met some other kids, also refugees, and we left the worrying to the adults. Worry is a stranger in the wonder world of kids. In recent years I have come to believe adults ought to be more like them.

Returning home, after the flood, was also an adventure; in the beginning at least. The water had been in all three of our houses but ours, setting lower than the others, was in the worst shape. The water had reached almost to the ceiling and the walls and floors were wet and muddy and smelly; a strange sort of odor. There was lots of cleaning to do but country houses, in that day, were constructed differently than today. There was no sheet rock to replace, no rewiring to be done, no fancy wallpaper to be stripped and re-done. All we had to do was scoop the mud out and scrub down the floors and walls and move back in.

Early in this account I told you that, when trying to deal with any problem, Daddy always found a way. Well, there was one little problem associated with our return after the flood in which Daddy's solution came near to killing or seriously injuring him. Our water supply was a pump mounted on a pipe sunk in the ground to a depth below the water table so the ground water could be pumped up. To the deepest section of the pipe was fitted a strainer with sieve-like perforations. This allowed the water to flow into the pipe while keeping unwanted particles out.

Having been under the flood's muddy waters for a month or more, the strainer was clogged with silt so no water could enter the pipe. As an alternative to pulling the entire assembly out of the ground to get to and clean the strainer, Daddy had a bright idea. The strainer was just a pipe with a bunch of holes, wasn't it? And a few more should only make it better, right? So why not just get the shotgun and fire a load of birdshot down the pipe? Congratulating himself on his brilliantly-conceived solution, Daddy banged away.

Wrong! He forgot that, when the gun was fired, the explosive gasses would have nowhere to go except to come back in his face, bringing up all manner of mud and whatever else had settled in the pipe.

Initially, we all thought that, at the least, he had blinded himself. There was so much mud and debris in his eyes, you couldn't even see his pupils and, of course, he couldn't see. But, Mama, like always, kept her wits about her. She had a bucket of clean water she had carried from a pump that had not been flooded. Using that, she bathed Daddy's eyes until they were clean and he could see again.

In the end there was no harm but it was a terrible fright and was one more reason we will never forget the '37 flood.

I guess the flood got Daddy to thinking for it wasn't too long after we moved back that he began planning to build us a new house. Some three hundred yards away there was another, larger ditch dump. It was much older so that the ditch from which it had been created had long since been filled with silt and it was an ideal location for a house; one where, if the flood came again, the house would be above it. Daddy planned to use our old house and the lumber from another that was sitting vacant to create an altogether new house. He sought and received the landowner's permission and set to work.

Rather than taking our old house down board by board, he planned to move the major part of it intact, with Grandpa's help, of course. The operation fascinated me as I watched, and, while I don't now recall all the details I know it went something like this. First, they cut several suitable logs to serve as rollers and located three or four of them under the house and, by knocking out the blocks it set on, lowered the house onto the rollers. They then hitched a team of mules to the house and pulled it forward a few feet until the rear-most roller was left behind. Then they unhitched the mules, hooked them up to the now-free roller and re-positioned it as the front roller. Again, they hooked up to the house and rolled it forward a few more feet. Over and over they repeated these steps until the house was in position in the new location.

Daddy tore down the other, uninhabited, house and proceeded to assemble the parts into our new house. We now had a three-room house in a very nice location. The front room served as the living room but it also contained a bed where Mama and Daddy slept. Behind it was a large bedroom where all us kids slept and, to one side, was a kitchen. A nice porch wrapped around the living room and there was a smaller one with doors to the kitchen and the back bedroom. Daddy knew where there was a large plot of wild-growing Bermuda grass and he used that to sod a good part of the front yard and down one side. He had picked a location with two cottonwood trees that now stood in our new front yard. Mama planted lots of flowers, including buttercups to line the path leading down to the road. When it was all finished, it was an altogether fine house for that time and place and we were all proud. It was after we moved in that Royce was born.

We were not only proud of our new house, we were proud of our daddy. Once again he had proved himself to be, not only a man of vision, but one with the ability and determination to turn his vision into reality.

But the winds that would blow our world away were already gathering.

27

The Year of Tragedy

Our family ended the year nineteen-thirty-seven on a mountain top, never suspecting that, just beyond, there waited the twisted canyons of despair. And I, unaware of what I was doing, was a part of it. I turned twelve that July. There was a girl in our school a few years older, about fourteen or fifteen and I carried notes to her. Notes from my daddy. And I brought her notes home to him.

All my life I have asked myself how I failed to see it; how a boy my age could have been so blind, but it never entered my mind that I was being used as a tool in the betrayal of my own Mama. I never thought to question the purpose of the notes and, of course, I never read them.

But Mama wasn't blind. One morning, when I was leaving for school, she called me back and asked if I had a note and I told her I did and she asked to see it. When I looked into her face as she read it I could see something was terribly wrong but I still didn't suspect what it was. She asked if there had been other notes and I said there had.

She gave the note back to me and told me to take it on and I did.

Not long after that there was a day my daddy didn't come home and the girl from school was missing. For a while we clung to a ledge of hope, dangling over the deep, dark canyon, feeling the ground crumble beneath our feet. And then the girl's mother said she had found a note, a note from her daughter. She had gone away with Daddy.

Eventually, Mama got a post card. Daddy and the girl were somewhere out west, California, I think. I have no idea what he wrote but his message was clear. It was goodbye.

Earlier, I have referred to, and quoted from, a book written by my brother. He wrote about the trials faced by our mother and he selected as a title, *Mama Never Cried*. But he was younger than I and didn't see the things I saw. Mama cried but she hid it. She knew that if the family was to survive, she had to be strong.

The Year of Tragedy

When Daddy left us, we had no money and very little in the way of food, but we had a huge pile of shattered dreams and a multitude of questions, unasked, for we didn't even know how to frame them.

The community's attitude toward us changed. I guess they just didn't know what to say; surely they didn't blame us; but they didn't say anything. All we got were strange looks. In the case of a death, neighbors know what do and they pitch in to help and comfort the survivors. But, for us, there was only their silence. Perhaps they hoped, as we did, that this bad dream would soon be over and everything would be as it was again.

I guess, deep down, I knew it would never be over. But, late one night, after he had been gone several months, I awoke to the sound of Mama talking quietly in the other room. And then I heard his voice and a great joy rose up in me. He was home and we wouldn't have to be alone any more.

I lay quiet and, after a while, Mama came in and roused us and she told us Daddy was home and wanted to see us. We went in to see him but the other kids were tired and still sleepy and didn't give him an enthusiastic greeting. And I didn't either. He had slipped away in the night and returned the same way. I was confused. How do you begin again?

We children soon went back to bed but I lay awake and I heard him say, "I thought they would be glad to see me but they didn't seem to care." And I wanted to say to him, "Daddy, I do care and I wanted you to care." But I didn't say it. I just lay silently in my bed and listened to the murmur of their voices until he left with the approaching dawn. Fearing the law, he had to get back across the river and into Missouri before daylight.

I think I knew the truth that night but hope didn't completely die until we learned, a few days later, the girl was pregnant. Her parents were adamant. If Daddy didn't marry her they would see him in the penitentiary. Mama held his freedom in her hands. She could have refused to grant him a divorce but she had a problem. Even knowing what he had done, she still loved him without reservation, as she had always done. She would rather set him free than see him in prison.

After many years I think I finally saw it; saw what Mama knew. When one has been wronged, forgiveness is knowing the cost the offender should pay and taking that cost upon yourself.

Daddy went free and Mama paid and she held no bitterness against him or against the girl. And neither do I. Mama taught me that.

After we knew Daddy was gone for good, Mama had to have someone to talk to. I was young but was old enough to understand some things and there was no one else. So we talked and we put together a plan for the immediate future. If we could, we would continue to work for Grandpa Weaver and live in the same house. I don't know what we would have done had he disagreed but he didn't and our course was set.

Looking back, I sometimes wonder if we would have had the courage to begin if we had known what lay ahead. I was twelve years old and she was twenty-eight and neither of us had any knowledge of how to manage our affairs. We were starting with absolutely no assets except our determination to succeed. So we began.

28

Getting on With Life

I don't know how long I went about in a daze but it seemed, then, like it was forever. Somehow my body continued to function but my mind was outside me, somewhere off in a different world. My head felt strange. I was two people. But we had to go on working and work helped me to hold on. I knew, as all of us did, that we had to work to survive as a family. There was no time to sit and let our minds wander; no time for self pity. There were things to be done and it was time for us to be getting on with life.

I knew that, as the oldest boy, I had to help Mama with family decisions.. The first full year we were alone, Mama and I tried to plan how we would survive the coming winter; how we would stay warm. Our house was heated by a stove that would burn wood or coal. But coal cost money. There was plenty timber for the cutting in the nearby woods but I, at twelve, and Vernon, at ten, just didn't have the strength or the skills to cut it. And, if we managed to get the trees down and trimmed up, we would have no means of hauling the logs home. So we made a deal with Grandpa. We agreed that Mama and me and Vernon would chop cotton for him the whole season and, in exchange, he would cut and haul our wood for the winter. It was our plan that Gene would stay home and care for the two younger ones, Lynn and Royce, leaving me and Vernon and Mama free to work.

All that long season, the three of us sweat up and down those long rows, under a burning sun, honoring our part of the contract. It was hard, laboring week after week with no pay day, but we went ahead, confident that one necessity was, thereby, being taken care of. We knew, before the year was out, we would need some cash money but we would have cotton picking time for that.

All the while we chopped Grandpa's cotton, Mama and I talked about other means, other arrangements, so we wouldn't have to do it this way again.

Then came the fall and time for Grandpa to fulfill his part of the contract and it hurts me, even now, to tell you he reneged. He just plain cheated us. Instead of a winter's supply of wood, he delivered just one lonely part wagon load of small poles, no more than a few weeks' supply, and none of them were cut into stove lengths.

That hurt. Lord, it hurt, just knowing our own grandpa had so little care for us. When Mama called him on it, pointing out the obvious fact, that we would require a lot more wood than that to get through the winter, Grandpa brushed her complaint aside, saying "Aw, pshaw!. That's enough wood." With tears in her eyes, Mama asked him, "Is all the work that these boys and I did for you worth no more than that?" But her tears touched no chord in him. She got no reply.

That was a hard lesson to learn but I guess we profited from it. It taught us what, I guess, we already knew; that if we were to survive we would have to do for ourselves. We couldn't depend on any one else. That knowledge didn't erase the pain but it gave us a new resolve, a new determination, to prove we could do what had to be done if we only worked together as a family. That's the way it was then, and the way it has always been. We have never found cause to change that philosophy.

When we saw where we stood with Grandpa, we bought a little bow saw, one that Vernon and I could handle, and we began to cut up the meager supply of poles Grandpa had left us. And then two things happened. A very kind man who had been watching us struggle came to help us, but not for long. When she saw what he was doing, his jealous wife came running and started an altercation with Mama, accusing her of trying to take her man from her when all he was trying to do was help two needful boys with a job that was too big for them. We loved him for trying but we understood why he wouldn't try again.

In the end, we took a few dollars needed for other things and bought some coal. A good neighbor, Mr. Oce Wolf, hauled it for us on his truck.

I feel, here, that I must get a few things said. Grandpa was not a cruel man. He was just plain stingy where money was concerned but, otherwise, was generous in giving us his time and consideration, yet he acknowledged no debt to us. He laughed with us. He joked with us. He guided us into an appreciation for music and taught us self-reliance. He generated in us a curiosity and a hunger for knowledge. Any successes we enjoyed later in life were, I believe, due in part to lessons we learned from him. But I still must ask how a caring man could do the thing I have just described to you. I've never understood it.

I guess, if I understood Grandpa, I could also understand Daddy for they seemed to have a similar philosophy as to children: enjoy them while they are in your presence, nurture and teach them; instruct them in the value of hard work and planning, and self-reliance and logical thought, but also make them understand they are an asset, yours to use as you see fit, and that you owe them nothing more.

No one owed us anything. Only one man, Mister Sam, ever went out of his way to help us and I have already told you about him. But he did it only because he was a good man; not because of any debt he owed us.

Today, persons in the position we were in would have access to a generous welfare program. But there were no such programs available to us then. There was a Red Cross place in the court house at Dyersburg and Mama and I went there once, but only once. The person who took us there did not do it as a charitable act. He charged us a dollar for gas.

When we got there, we felt the staff treated us like beggars and they only offered us some half-rotten fruit. Maybe that was the best they could do but just being there depressed me and I could tell Mama felt the same. When we got home, I said to Mama, "I don't know about you but I don't ever want go back there unless we get awful hungry." When she heard me say that I could see her face light with a great relief. The sadness seemed to disappear to be replaced by happiness and she said, "Son, I am glad you said that for I don't want to go back either and I don't think we will have to. We'll do it on our own." And within me I sensed a gladness I hadn't felt for a long time. We were going to make it. It wasn't going to be easy but, if we worked together, we were going to make it.

These times I have spoken of were hard and, even now, as I pull them from my memory, I sense again a wisp of the pain of abandonment and betrayal. But with those memories comes also the knowledge that these are the things that molded me and made me who I am. They prepared me for life in a world where right does not always triumph; where goodness is not always rewarded nor evil punished, and they taught me that we have the power and the duty to forge our own destiny. Struggle made me strong and it imbedded in me one principle from which I will never depart. I vow never to knowingly and deliberately wrong another human being. Never.

Now, it's time to put these things behind and go on to better memories. I will write no more of sadness.

Gradually, at our house, we returned to a state near normalcy. We were getting by. Our neighbors no longer felt discomfort in our presence. Our young friends soon forgot their prying questions. Wounds healed and we turned our eyes to the future and put away things that were past.

29

Broadmoor, its Character and its Characters

I'm not going to try to tell you about everybody on Broadmoor but there are a couple more I want to mention. First, there was Mr. Dudley. I don't recall, in that time, that I ever knew his first name. The adults just called him Dud.

He had an old, flat bed truck that he drove conservatively. Make that *very* conservatively. For instance, once a group of us boys had walked up to Bee-Varm and were headed home when we saw Mr. Dudley coming in his truck. We all stood beside the road and put a thumb up but Mr. Dudley didn't stop. He didn't even slow down. He just kept on churning. Well, we weren't so easily put off. As he passed us we simply ran him down and clambered up on the truck and enjoyed a free, but leisurely, ride to Broadmoor.

Mr. Dudley was a great story teller. He was a pipe smoker and he made full use of that when he began to speak. At critical points in his story he would pause and give his full attention to the pipe. He would slowly pack it, then fumble through first one pocket then another for a match and, when he found one, the tobacco never lit on the first try. He would puff and suck and strike more matches and, finally, when his audience was about ready to seize him and say "Get on with it! What happened next?" he would let out a big billow of smoke and ask, "Now, where was I?"

Dud told this story about a catfish. A big catfish. I don't guarantee I'm telling it like he did, but, as I remember, the story went something like this.

There was a place Dud used to live when he was younger and, in coming and going, he had to cross a good-sized stream that flowed through the woods. He crossed on a foot log and, just downstream from where he crossed, there was a fairly large pool, about waist deep. It looked like the pool was in a hollow that remained when a large tree was uprooted some years ago. The flowing waters made an eddy in the hollow and that was probably what caused the pool to form.

Everybody knows it is in such a place that large catfishes like to lay up. There they don't have to go out searching for food. They just lay there, gaping mouth open, while the swirling waters bring the food to them and they just get fatter and fatter.

Well, Dud began to notice that, as he was crossing the stream, he would sometimes hear a faint sound, sort of like a grunt or a groan. In the beginning he dismissed it, assuming it was two tree limbs rubbing together as they moved in the wind. Then he noticed two things. The sound didn't come from above and he heard it on calm days same as he did when it was windy. That got his curiosity up and, at last, by careful observation, he traced the origin of the sound to the pool. Determined, now, to see the end of a mystery, he walked a few paces downstream, where the light was right, and stared into the pool. There was nothing there except for a large, water-soaked log laying on the bottom. And then, as a ray of sunshine penetrated the water, everything came clear. While he watched, he saw this log had fins that were moving lazily in the water.

Lord-a-mercy! That had to be the biggest catfish he had ever seen!

He could have let the big fish alone but a man born to hunt, like Dud was, can't do that and he began to plan how he was going to take him. It would do no good to try to hook him. In the first place, he had neither hook nor line strong enough to hold the fish. Hoggin' was out of the question. (Some people call it grappling, but down South it's hoggin'. What you do is, a bunch of men will enter a stream and move quietly along it, feeling in any hollow that might hold a fish and, when they find one, they gently slip a finger in its gills and toss it out on the bank.) This fish was way too big for that. Dud doubted he could even lift him with both hands if he was standing on dry land. So he continued to scheme and, at last, settled on a plan.

He couldn't take the fish by hoggin' but he could use some of those techniques. If you are gentle and make your approach slowly, you can touch, even pet, a big catfish without scaring him. So Dud began, almost every day, to ease himself into the pool and pet the fish and the fish didn't seem to mind. In fact, he seemed to get accustomed to it and enjoy it.

Then, when he thought the fish was ready, Dud got Uncle Ed to help him. They brought the mule and a rope and a ground slide and quietly approached the stream. Dud built a noose in the rope on the opposite end from the one hooked up to the mule and, dragging the rope with him, eased up to the fish and slipped the noose around him just back of the gills and pulled it kinda snug. Slowly, after Dud got clear, Uncle Ed eased the mule forward until the rope tightened.

And when that fish began to understand he was caught he near splashed that pool dry! Jumpin' around; tail slashin'; throwin' his head one way and then another and the mule hunkered down and, while it was doubtful at first, the mule finally drug him out on the bank and, Lord! Weren't that a fish! Dud, him and Uncle Ed, they rassled the fish up on the slide and tuck him home. Before they cleaned him and cut him up they sent the kids to tell the neighbors to come and see him. They wanted to weigh him but all they had was some cotton scales and they only went up to a hundred and forty and that wouldn't touch this fish.

And they did have theirselves a fish fry! Meat was a little strong, though.

Everybody believed Dud but he brought up the subject of provenance anyway. Unfortunately, Uncle Ed had long since gone on and all the others who saw the fish before he was et had moved off down the river. But nobody doubted Dud.

"Biggest catfish I ever seen," he said.

Speaking of storytellers, I've got to go back to Bo for a moment. He was a good 'un. Mark Twain had no edge on him. He could draw you in so deep there was no way out before he ever let you in on the fact that what you were hearing happened only in his imagination.

He loved doing that to his wife. Marcene was no dummy but, after being victimized by him for years, she would still fall for one of his lines. When he would start, Marcene would say, "Now, Bo, you know that's not true." But he could always convince her that, this time, he spoke the truth.

Once he asked her if she had heard about the new invention, the water melon thumper, they had come up with. Of course, she began, "Now, Bo" but he assured her he was not kidding. He explained. He reminded her that the most reliable way to judge whether a water melon is ripe is to thump it, but it takes a lot of time to thump a whole field full of water melons by hand. The new machine, he told her, attaches to a tractor and it thumps all the water melons as it passes through the field. It's much faster.

Marcene started out doubting but ended up believing and she didn't even know she had been had again until later when she tried to explain the new invention to someone else.

Another Bo loved to get hooked on one of his lines was his little sister, my own dear wife-to-be, Peg. This was one of his best. It was winter and a sudden cold spell hit. Temperatures plunged overnight and the watering pond for the livestock froze over.

There was a barbed wire fence running across one end of the pond. One strand was above the surface and one was lower, now visible but below the ice. That was enough for Bo.

He came in from the cold, shucked his gloves, and backed up to the stove in a room where Peg and others sat, and he said, "Man! It's cold out there." And he let that lay a moment and continued. "The pond is plumb froze over." He paused again and followed up, "Come up so quick it froze the shadow of the fence right into the ice!" Peg, who had been only half listening, now came fully alert and she asked, "Bo, what did you say?" and he repeated, "Shadow of the fence froze right into the ice." This, Peg had to see. So she got her coat and her heavy shoes on and Bo took her out and showed her the proof. There, plain for all to see, was one strand of wire and, below, frozen solidly into the ice, was its shadow.

To this day, Peg still won't say whether she really believed that.

Now, since I have already brought her name up again, I had better tell you a little about Peg. When we moved to Broadmoor she was just a baby and I was about eight years old. The first time ever I saw her I was, for some reason, at their house and she was on the porch playing with a doll. I thought, then, she was just the cutest little thing. And the years passed and I saw her now and then but paid scant attention to the little girl she had become.

Then I grew up and, in nineteen forty-five, went into the navy. By the time I came home more than two years later, Peg was a teenager, near to being grown, and I thought she was still just the cutest little thing. Still, it was a couple of years before I had the nerve to ask her out and she accepted. Then, there came the night we stood by her front gate and I asked her to marry me, and, again, she accepted.

June 6, 1952, was, I still believe, the date we set but that was like a lot of other days in our lives. Confused, that is. At that time I was in the air force, stationed at Smyrna, Tennessee, which is near Nashville, several hours' travel time from Broadmoor. We would only have the weekend and so we planned for me to pick her up and take her to Mississippi, just below Memphis, where getting married was easy and quick.

When I arrived at her door, there sat Peg, barefooted and wearing what was obviously not her wedding gown and she asked, "What are you doing here?" When I stammered out an explanation, she said, "It's tomorrow. We're supposed to get married tomorrow!" And there I stood, in my dress uniform and with a rented car and my two dollars for the license and it was not today. It was tomorrow!

But we didn't argue. She quickly got herself ready and we set out on what would be the rest of the most momentous day of my life.

That was more than fifty years ago. We've had good years and bad. Peg has faithfully and willingly followed me from Tennessee to Illinois, to Texas, to Oklahoma and to Oregon and back to Alabama and I believe, all along, we have agreed on one thing. Whether it was supposed to be today or it was tomorrow, the day we got married was the right day.

We have shared a lot of years, Peg and Me, and we have seen a lot of changes. We produced seven remarkable children and watched them grow up. We've seen the seasons come and go and our hair is of a different hue. But when I look in a mirror I still see a vestige of the country boy from Broadmoor that once I was. And Peg? In my eyes, she's still the little girl with the doll, the teenager I admired, the woman who agreed to marry me and bear my children and the one who has stood always beside me and, you know what? She's still just the cutest little thing.

30

Drankin'

Let us say at the outset that we had some hesitancy at the thought of including this chapter in our book. As you read further, you will find that I, Bueford, later in my life, became a preacher. And, as you might expect, I am generally agin' drankin'. I know there are many who drink some in moderation and find no sin or shame in it and I have no argument with that, that is, *if* it is done in moderation and without harm to others. But, if I were to make a sermon of this, I would point out that therein lies the rub. There are few who imbibe that do not, at some time and some place, find themselves in violation of that "no harm to others" clause. But this is not a sermon and I will now leave this issue to your conscience and we will get on with our story.

Drankin' was not, I believe, a problem on Broadmoor but it was and is a part of Broadmoor lore. Some drankin' did occur but there were firm, though unwritten, rules. The first rule was that *nobody* did it at home. Nobody kept a cold six-pack in their icebox or a little sippin' whiskey in the cabinet.

Let me amplify that. No husband would have been *permitted* to do so. Any wife finding alcohol in the house would, without hesitation, have poured it out, satisfied that what she did was for sake of her errant husband's soul. Local religious beliefs, as practiced then, allowed for no use of alcohol under any circumstances. Even in church, when they took the Lord's Supper, they substituted plain grape juice for the wine.

Now I'm not saying no drankin' ever took place at all. It just was not done at home. But there were some in the community who would occasionally go out and take on a load and that sometimes produced a story to be told and repeated and laughed about You might find a few of them amusing..

There was, for instance, this one guy. (I will omit his name and call him MP.) One Saturday night he was sitting in a joint up on Reelfoot when the Lake

County cops came looking for suitable guests they might invite to their place for the weekend and, for transportation, they had brought along a van which they backed up to the front door.

One of the officers approached the table where Milllard—Sorry, I mean MP—sat and asked, "Hey, buddy. You been drinking?" (Apparently the cop hadn't noticed all those empties covering the table top.) When MP acknowledged he had had a couple, the cop asked, "Well, can you walk?" To which MP answered honestly, "Why, officer, I been walking since I was two years old!" Whereupon, the cop, who failed to see the humor in this, said to MP, "Well, let's see you get up and walk out there and get in that van." So that's how MP qualified for a free night's lodging.

When he told about it later, MP said the cops probably did him a favor. Had they not come along, he said, odds are he would have stayed on there and got drunk.

Even some in our own family were known to take a nip from time to time. This next story became a part of the family legend.

Grandma Weaver had, for weeks, been nagging at Grandpa asking that, the next time he went to town, he go by and pick her up a new rain barrel.

There was this manufacturing plant in Dyersburg that used materials shipped to them in nice oaken barrels and, when they were empty, they would sell them to the public at a reasonable price, something less than a dollar each.

There was a day Grandpa came in from town, still empty handed, barrel-wise, but with a small bottle in his pocket and the hint of alcohol on his breath. Of course, Grandma lit into him, "Bill, what have you been drinking? (and before he could deny it) Don't you deny it! I can smell it on your breath!"

Grandpa had no choice but to admit he had picked up a little wine and, when Grandma demanded to know how much and what it cost, he sheepishly owned up to spending seventy-five cents for a pint.

Well, that really set Grandma off. She threw her dishrag down and her hands in the air and cried, "Seventy-five cents? *Seventy-five cents?* Why, Bill, you could have got a *barrel* for that!" at which Grandpa sprang to his feet, reaching for his hat and the doorknob, while earnestly beseeching Grandma, "Lord, tell me where, Cass, where?"

It's a well-known fact that one who has been drankin' will sometimes let his mouth overload another part of his anatomy. There was this night when a carload of Broadmoor boys, one of whom was Harvey H., had been out lifting a few and were driving down a country road while Harvey and JW, who was known for his strong body and hard head, were sniping at each other. It reached the point where JW proposed that the driver stop and he would get out and give Harvey a whuppin'. To which Harvey responded, "Well, why don't we just find out if you can!"

When the accommodating driver reached a suitable spot, he pulled over and the two got out in the moonlight and squared off and, with one clean punch, Harvey laid JW in the ditch. Then, after giving him a moment to recover, he and the others picked JW up, brushed him off and helped him back into the car and they drove on.

The sniping stopped but they hadn't gone much more than a mile when JW (he of the hard head) said to Harvey, "I don't believe you can do that again." So once more the driver stopped; the boys got out and squared off and, with one clean punch, Harvey laid JW in the ditch!

Again, they loaded up and drove on to the next beer joint where, it having been established to the satisfaction of all whether JW could or could not administer the promised whuppin', Harvey and JW spent the remainder of the evening buying each other beer.

Later, on the way home, they stopped on a deserted stretch of road and all got out to commune with nature and were about to get back in the car when JW broke the silence: "Harve?—," and, as Harve turned expectantly, JW sighed and said, "Oh, never mind." And they all got in the car and went home.

One more:

A different group of boys, this time including our brother Vernon, after having had one or two, were wending their way home one dark night. They had taken a shortcut on a narrow dirt road when Vernon shouted, "Stop! Stop! I gotta go! I gotta go *now*!" Having learned from past experience that when Vernon put it that way he really meant it, the driver came to an immediate stop in the middle of the road, and, as soon as the wheels stopped turning, Vernon flung the door open, took one step, and was swallowed up in the darkness. Then, a split second later, there came a loud splash from somewhere below and that was followed by an equally loud string of cuss-words, some invented on the spot!

When the others cautiously investigated, they discovered the truth. In his haste to accommodate Vernon, the driver had failed to warn him that he had stopped on a narrow, rail-less bridge over a muddy creek ten feet below!

That wasn't the only time in his lifetime that Vernon was known to have one too many but it was, without doubt, the quickest he ever sobered up.

With that one, I will leave the subject of Drankin'. I trust you will not presume that, by telling these stories and joining in the laughter, I am signaling an endorsement of the practice. I don't recommend it but the decision is between you and your conscience.

31

Waltie

You had to look below the surface to know Waltie.

At first glance, you saw him as a meek, mild mannered person. But, on closer observation, you became aware he had an inner strength which surpassed that of ordinary men. He held firm convictions about how life should be lived and he lived by his convictions.

Every community needs a conscience and Waltie served that purpose for Broadmoor.

He was an elder in the Church of Christ that sat across the highway from the store. I don't know all the tenets of that Church but there was never any doubt in anyone's mind that Waltie practiced what his Church preached and did so from a sincere and honest heart.

As I understood it, the Church taught that an individual had to partake of the Lord's Supper every Sunday and, if he missed a Sunday and died before he had another opportunity to partake of it, he was condemned to hell. I wondered if there was any circumstance that would permit a breach of that rule. What about a life and death situation?

So I asked him, "If some Sunday you were crossing the road on your way to church and you saw a man who had been hit by a car. You knew that if you stopped and helped him he would live but you would miss the Lord's Supper. You also knew he would die if you did not help him. What would you do?"

Without hesitation, he said, "I would go to Church."

Of course, what he should have said was that he didn't have time to respond to foolish questions from the likes of me. But, instead, he answered honestly in terms of what he believed God's word teaches. One may disagree with him if he wants to, but if, in fact, that is God's word on the subject, Waltie was right.

Man ought to always obey the word of God.

Waltie set standards for himself and never wavered from them. To him, honesty and integrity were not negotiables. There came a time, while I was away in the navy, that Mama and the younger kids moved away to Arkansas and, after a month or so, she got a letter from Waltie. In balancing his books, he had discovered a small error. He had short-changed her in a transaction and he wanted to apologize for it. It was only a matter of a few cents, not much more than the cost of the postage, but there in the envelope, taped to a card, was every cent he owed her.

Waltie had two daughters in whom he delighted. Of the two, Metha, the oldest, was quieter and more subdued. (I do have information from a reliable source that, when among close friends, she was lots of fun.) Then there was Sue, a mere baby when I first knew her and Waltie would sometimes let her come downstairs and stay with him in the store for a while. Sue was then a gamine, an elf, a playful fairy, a ray of light in a darkened room, and, when those sparkling brown eyes hit you with their mischievous gleam and that lilting little giggle broke forth, she captivated every heart; especially that of her daddy.

Over the years I have remembered Waltie. He was not satisfied with goals for his life that did not require excellence. He would settle for nothing less than perfection; perfect purity of thought and deed. Many others would lower the bar with a shrug of the shoulders and say, "nobody's perfect," but not Waltie.

I admired him for that.

I don't know if he attained his goals but one thing I do know is that his life is an example and a challenge to we who followed him. God's word admonishes us to be perfect as He is perfect. To lower the bar is not acceptable to God or man and Waltie's life is a resounding Amen to that truth.

Waltie was a good man.

32

A Date That Will Live in Infamy

December 7, 1941. Sunday. A quiet day of rest on Broadmoor in Dyer County, Tennessee. I was fourteen years old and was vaguely aware there was a war going on in Europe and Asia but I wasn't disturbed by that knowledge. I didn't even know where Europe and Asia was.

Then Grandpa's call broke the silence. Always, when he wanted to attract the attention of the rest of us, he would come out on his porch and holler, "Whoop, Whoop!" and we knew he had something to tell us and we would come running.

That day he had been listening to a news broadcast when it was interrupted by the announcement that Japan had attacked and destroyed our naval forces tied up at Pearl Harbor. It was no joke. Many of our men had been killed. We were at war. Like most Americans on that day, we wondered where Pearl Harbor was, but Grandpa knew and he told us.

I still had some difficulty getting my mind around the matter and I suspect the others did too, but we all spoke in hushed tones. I guess the adults, better than me, understood what this was going to do to the peaceful, untroubled existence we had, until then, enjoyed.

We knew about the draft and the registration of our menfolk but we knew no one who had yet been inducted. That was going to change. Pretty soon, familiar faces began to disappear.

Ellis Eaton went early. So did Leland Weaver, one of Grandpa's nephews who had been staying with him. Homer Chandler, a family friend from Bogota was gone. Across the river, Mama's brother, Ernest, and, a little later, Moody, were called up. Soon, we missed Calvin Pilkenton and Hub Henderson, Mr. Slim's nephew. Clifford Hood could have waited for the draft but he volunteered and the next time we saw him he was wearing jump boots and paratrooper wings.

A major B-17 training base was established at Dyersburg and the streets began to be filled with men in uniform. Some older men, not exposed to the draft, moved their families away from Broadmoor to take jobs that were a part of the war effort. Popular destinations were Detroit and Chicago.

To us, every service man was a hero. One event in particular proved that. It was a Saturday night at Ridgely and some of the boys from the air base were in town and a little rowdy and the local police picked some of them up and threw them in jail. When that news hit the street, some two hundred people (for Ridgely, that was a major part of the population) surrounded the jail, demanding their release. A standoff developed and the crowd grew impatient and louder.

One pseudo-tough cop was heard to say, "I ought to just pull out this gun and start shootin'" and a voice came from the crowd, "Just remember the gun you're totin' wasn't the last one they made!" That crowd was ready to go to war to secure the release of "their" boys.

Fortunately, a more level head prevailed and called the base MP's. They responded and the airmen were released to their custody.

For most of the war the Broadmoor luck held and we had to endure no military funerals. No one came home with parts missing. But the war wore on until, finally, my contemporaries; school friends a year or so older than me, began to hear the call. The army took Willard Johnson and Don Parker and, from Cuckleburr, Glenn Boswell and Ralph Sanford. J. C. Buchanan joined the navy. When I reached eighteen, I, myself, went navy. I was lucky and saw the war's end while still in boot camp.

But, somewhere along the way, our luck ran out.

Ralph Sanford became our first and only fatality. Any such loss would have been hard to bear but Ralph's story, as I heard it, seemed to me to be particularly tragic. Ralph was on a troopship, headed for Europe, when it was torpedoed in the North Atlantic. He was one of the fortunate ones who found a spot in a life raft. He, and those with him, were alive but without food and water. They drifted for several days and then a search plane spotted them. They began to wave and cheer and, in the excitement, Ralph fell overboard and, by that time, was so weakened he couldn't climb back in. Neither did the others have the strength to pull him in. Ralph hung on for a while but, before the rescue ship came, he let go and drifted away.

I wept for my friend, not yet twenty, who died having never had a chance to live. But I know my pain was as nothing compared to that of his mother.

The local newspaper then regularly featured a poet's corner. One poem appeared there under the name of Ralph's mother. Most of it is gone from my memory and only a part of one couplet remains. In its first line, she wrote something of *"...battles to be won."* Then the rhyming line: *"And on the sea at midnight, I gave my darling Son."* In those few words I think I can see something of all the pain of all the mothers who lost sons in that tragic and useless war.

Glenn Boswell, slightly older but in the same class as me in school, came home with two artificial legs. It was his first day in combat and, under an artillery attack, he dived for a foxhole and nearly made it before an exploding round amputated both his legs below the knee.

Later, he wrote to me from the hospital before he had got his prostheses and he was really down. They had told him he would be able to walk again but he didn't believe that. Others on his ward were having a hard time with theirs.

Then, not long after, I heard from him again and was very excited. Proudly, he wrote, "I walked today!" He said, "I had to hold onto somebody for help but I walked and now I know I can do it."

I was in the navy when Glenn finally came home but I was able to see him and talk to him a few times when I was on leave in October of that year and, also, later, after I completed my navy hitch. I guess I was expecting, or at least hoping, Glenn would be the same happy, fun-loving boy I knew in school. But he wasn't. It seemed to me he was too much aware that others were aware he was walking on artificial legs. He would make little jokes about them, perhaps intended to ease the others' discomfort, but all his jokes came off sounding a little hollow.

Both Glenn and I moved away and we lost track of each other. I have thought of him over the years and have hoped he found other friends and that he came to accept his condition and was able to make a new life for himself. I truly hope so.

Don Parker had a different kind of a war story. All his life he had been a sleep walker. I mean he would get out of bed and take real walks and never know it. It was strange, for some of the other brothers in his family did the same thing. They lived in a house surrounded by woods and, with some frequency, one or the other of them would wake up standing on some woodland path, wondering where he was and how he got there.

Anyway, after Don was assigned to a combat unit, but one not yet engaged, they found him, on several occasions, walking, sound asleep, about the lines at night and they sent him back to a hospital for observation. A doctor certified he was suffering from battle fatigue and sent him to the rear. Don thought the doctor's diagnosis was amusing, seeing as how he had never been in a battle.

Willard (Hunt) Johnson was taken prisoner by the Germans soon after he arrived in the combat zone. I don't recall how long he was imprisoned but I do remember it was for a considerable time and his family, with no word from him, began to lose hope he would ever return. When, in time, he did come home, his family, and the entire community greeted him with unabashed joy.

Gene was there that day and he recently wrote this about it.

> His real name was Willard but most of us called him Hunt. We don't know where that nick name came from but that's what we called him. The Johnsons, Miz Preble and Mr. Jim, had nine children and Hunt was the oldest boy. It was World War II and Hunt came of draft age sometime in 1944. When his name reached the top of the list, things began to happen fast. Hunt was quickly called up, given a minimum of infantry training and a short visit home and then he was gone; shipped out for Europe and combat.
>
> It seemed to us he had hardly gone and we had only begun to realize we missed him when the telegram came. First he was missing in action, then a prisoner of war and, after that, as the months dragged by with no word, his family's hopes began to fade. His mother didn't talk about it but we could read in her eyes the burden of pain she carried. Mr. Jim became convinced his boy was dead and he said we shouldn't expect to see Hunt on Broadmoor again.
>
> And the weeks and months stretched out and the rest of the community began to feel Mr. Jim was probably right.
>
> Then one warm day in the late spring of '45 the two o'clock bus that almost never stopped at Broadmoor pulled over at the entrance to the dirt road that led down to the Johnson house and a lone figure dropped off. At first, those gathered and watching at the store stared in hope but in disbelief. At that distance they couldn't be sure, but finally one of them dared to speak the words that were straining for birth in each mind: "Oh, my Lord! It's him! It's Hunt! He ain't dead; it's Hunt and he has come home!"
>
> And from there, like wildfire, the word went out across the community. On Broadmoor there were no telephones or any other means of public communication but somehow the words seemed to generate a power of their own as they leaped from mouth to mouth: "Hunt's home! Hunt's home! We just saw him. He ain't dead, he's home!"
>
> And they all came. On foot, in cars, on mule-back and by bicycle. From every direction and by every means they came; every living soul on Broadmoor. In ones and twos and in larger groups, they descended upon the Johnson house eager to share in their joy. They found Hunt sitting in a chair on the front porch, close beside his beaming mother, and with all his brothers and sisters crowding around him, grinning, crying, touching him and hanging on to his every word. All, that is, but Leland. Leland was then about sixteen

and, earlier in the day, he had caught a ride up to Ridgely and didn't know yet.

As the afternoon wore on and each new visitor arrived, Hunt would step down and meet them in the yard where he would hug or shake hands with the adults and would ruffle the hair of the kids.

From the house we could see where the dirt road came off the highway, about a half-mile away and, at that distance, could recognize each community member as they approached and a question began to build, "Will the next one be Leland?"

Then, at last, a figure on foot turned off the highway and headed down the dirt road and there was no question who it was. At first, his gait was a brisk walk. Then he broke into a trot and Hunt got to his feet and stepped down from the porch and the trot became a lope and, finally, as Hunt walked out to meet his brother, Leland was coming on at a dead run.

As the whole gathered community watched, brother and brother met at the edge of the yard and threw their arms around each other and held on tight and if any word was spoken, either by them or by those watching the scene through weeping eyes, no one could later say. In any event, words were unnecessary. None were required to set that moment forever in our memory. The moment said it all.

Hunt Johnson had come home.

As the fighting came to an end; first in Europe and then in the Pacific, others began to come home, one by one. None of them talked much about the war. I heard Calvin Pilkenton came home with a Silver Star but I don't know if that's true for I never heard him speak of it. If others earned medals they kept that knowledge to themselves.

The war was over and Broadmoor would never be the same.

33

Leaving Broadmoor

At the end of 1945, while I was away in the navy, and Broadmoor was still viable, Mama decided it was time to leave the place that had been our home for more than ten years. Royce was born and Gene and Lynn had grown to adolescence there and Vernon and I had become young men. Our time at Broadmoor had brought us both happiness and sorrow but, in leaving, we carried with us only light hearts and pleasant memories.

Mama left, principally, in the hope of providing Gene, now ready for high school, and the younger boys, better educational prospects than I had found. She settled the family in a little community called Mandalay, near Manila, Arkansas, on a farm operated by her brother, our Uncle Jesse. The bus to the local grade school and to the high school at Manila, passed by our front door.

After I left the navy in October of 1947, I joined Mama and the kids. We found there many good and gracious people but, when we thought of home, it was still the picture of Broadmoor that came to our minds.

Later, in 1951, with Gene then in the army, the family moved to Memphis and, for the first time in our lives, we earned our living by means other than farm labor.

34

Mama

For the next twelve or fourteen years after leaving Broadmoor, first in Arkansas and later at Memphis, Mama maintained a home for the family. A part of that time one or more of us boys were away in military service. Eventually, each of us married and established our own homes.

About 1960, with no continuing family responsibilities, Mama left her long-time job at the Baptist Hospital in Memphis and sought more satisfying employment. For a year or so, she served as a house mother in a children's home near Memphis. She stayed a time with Vernon, then in Wichita, caring for his children while he and Wilma worked. For some two years she was back in Arkansas, living with and assisting her sister, Ruth. She accepted a job at Huntsville, Alabama (Both Lynn and I then lived near there) helping a widowed father care for his motherless children and, later, when he re-married, she took a similar position in Anniston. When that father also found a wife, she went to live with Gene in College Park, Georgia. There, she established a clientele of families she served by going into their homes and caring for the children while the parents were away. She did that for many years before she moved to Arab, Alabama, where Lynn and I arranged a nice, private apartment for her. She lived there until she moved to Paris, Tennessee, where Royce had built for her a private suite attached to his house. There she remained until advancing years required she have closer care than we could give and she moved back to Alabama, again near Lynn and me, and into a personal care facility. Mama remained there until December, 1999, when she died, just seventeen days short of her ninetieth birthday.

35

Vernon

Vernon, over the years, worked at many jobs and in many places, including Dyersburg and Memphis, Tennessee; Detroit and Flint, Michigan; Chicago; Wichita; the Houston, Texas area; South Louisiana, and many others. Much of his working career was spent pulling the big rigs across the highways of the country, coast to coast.

In his younger years, he served two hitches in the army, serving much of the first one in Korea and the latter in Germany.

Vernon first married Wilma Arrington of Ridgely and, together, they had four children. The first child, Edwin, died almost immediately after birth. Robert, the youngest, died after he was well into adulthood. Wilma has also been gone for some years. Rebecca and Ronald, still live.

Vernon later married Eva Pearl Bissell (former wife of Oren) and, still later, his last wife, Geraldine. Neither of the later marriages produced any children.

In the fall of 1989, Vernon succumbed to heart failure at the VA hospital in Memphis and was buried at a cemetery outside Dyersburg.

36

Gene

Gene, after graduation from high school at Manila, Arkansas, went into the army in 1951. His major duty assignment was as an infantryman and paratrooper in the 82nd Airborne Division at Fort Bragg, North Carolina. After the army he settled in Memphis, where Mama then lived, and where he worked at several jobs before going to work as a clerk in the Post Office in 1956. In 1963, he secured an appointment as a Postal Inspector and spent the next twenty years doing postal related investigations, mostly of criminal matters, across the nation, but mostly in the Southeastern States. He retired in 1983 and, since that time, has lived in College Park, Georgia.

In 1959, Gene married Joann Smith of Corning, Arkansas and she bore him three children, Laura, Wally and Jamie. At this writing, he has four grandchildren. To his great sorrow, shared by all of us, Joann left this life in February, 2001.

Gene has written and published two previous books; *Mama Never Cried*, a memoir of our mother, and *For One Brief Moment*, in which he writes of Joann and of the courage she showed and of the loving support of her friends during her final illness.

37

Lynn

Born at Bogota, Lynn was only a few months old when the family moved to Broadmoor and he was eleven when they moved on to Arkansas where they lived in the little cross-roads community of Mandalay. He attended the nearby Milligan Ridge elementary school and, later, the high school at Manila where he completed the tenth grade in 1951. That same year he, Mama and Royce moved to Memphis where, rather than entering school, Lynn went to work for the Memphis Street Railway Company. There (the way he proudly puts it) he had vaulted up the ladder and was drawing down nearly a dollar an hour when he threw away that promising career and moved with Joe Smith, a school chum from Arkansas, to Flint, Michigan, where he accepted a position in the automotive construction industry. (That is to say he got work on the assembly line for the Fisher Body Division of General Motors.)

In mid-1953, having exhausted himself installing windshields in Chevys, he returned to Broadmoor and lived with and worked for Cheat and Aunt Reldie through that summer and fall and, in January of the next year, he entered the army along with Perchworthy James from Broadmoor, Bobby Boswell from Cuckleburr and Joe Bennett from Bogota. Unfortunately, after basic training at Ft. Gordon, GA, Perchworthy was separated from the group but the other three went, together, to artillery training at Ft. Bliss, Texas where, except for two months of temporary duty at Ft. Huachuca, Arizona, they remained for their entire hitch and until their discharge in January, 1956.

In notes recently made for this history brief, Lynn wrote: "I will always be thankful for having Boswell and Bennett with me while I was in the army for they became two friends I will never forget."

Leaving the army more career oriented than before, Lynn went to work in Memphis at the Air Force's Mallory Depot as an IBM tabulating machine operator and was later moved up to a project planning position.

Two years later he met and married Mary Elizabeth Beason. (Mary has always been called, familiarly, Mary Tom and that is somehow related to the fact that her father's name was Tom.) Together they have had two children, Carol Lynn and Gene Wesley.

In 1963, with Mallory in the process of being closed, Lynn and family moved to Battle Creek, Michigan, where he continued to work for the government and trained as a computer programmer.

The next year, 1964, they moved permanently back south, where Lynn worked as a computer programmer, and later as supervisor of a programming group for the Army Missile Command at Redstone Arsenal, Huntsville, Alabama.

He and Mary Tom took up residence in the town of Arab, Alabama where they still live today.

Lynn retired from his government job in 1993 but worked for another seven years doing essentially the same thing as a contractor before finally ending his working career in August of 2000.

Lynn masquerades as a simple, country boy but when someone sees beyond his blue jeans, flannel shirt, CAT hat and the "Roll Tide" bumper sticker on his pickup and spots him for the suave, man of the world he truly is, he is ready with an explanation. He tells them (and it is all true.) it is due to the cosmopolitan lifestyle he has lived.

You see, he was born in BOGOTĂ, lived several of his formative years in MANDALAY, attended secondary school in MANILA, has lived many years among the ARABIANS and is fluent in their language and all its dialects and, several times a year, he visits PARIS. (that is, Paris, Tennessee, where Royce, our younger brother, lives.)

"How much more a man of the world can one be?" he asks as he lifts his plug of Red Man, pinkie delicately extended, and bites off a chew.

38

Royce

Royce was born at Broadmoor and was only eight when the family moved away. His memories of Broadmoor are few and mostly of childhood things but, in deference to his youth, he being only sixty-six at this writing, we will let him tell his own story in his own words. So, go ahead Royce. You got the floor.

Royce:
I am going to begin with a couple of kid-type stories which may not be of any great interest to you, the reader, but this may well be my only opportunity to memorialize them in print so I am going to take it.

There was this kid (and I don't even now recall his name) who was new to the neighborhood when one day he came to visit and play with me. We were both only about seven years old. The two of us had wandered down the dump into a wooded area when the boy turned to me and said something like, "Here comes a bear!" And he must have had the makings of a good actor for, when he said that, he became one. Spreading his up-raised arms, extending his claw-like fingers, opening his mouth wide and emitting a very convincing growl, he began to advance upon me. Well, his act was just too good. I had never seen a bear before but this sure looked like one to me and I had heard stories about how bears like to eat kids.

I didn't hesitate but instinctively raised the stick I was carrying and, with considerable force, rapped the charging bear between the eyes!

Did you ever see a bear cry? Well, this one did and he said, "Well, if you don't like me, I'll just go home!" And he did and I don't recall that he ever came back, neither the kid nor the bear.

There was the time that Buddy Green, along with his mother, Miss Annie Lou, had come to visit. As she sat down with Grandma to catch up on the neighborhood gossip, me and Buddy and Lynn went out to play. With his mother's words, "Buddy, don't you go climbing no trees!" still ringing in our ears, we went out to climb some trees.

One of our best climbing trees was a persimmon, the lowest limbs of which must have been a good ten or twelve feet above the ground and that is the one Buddy chose. He shinnied up rather briskly and was standing on the lowest limb, gripping the next highest one with both hands, when he inched out a little too far and both limbs snapped.

I can still picture Buddy, in perfect imitation of Wile E. Coyote (I see it in slow motion.) riding the limbs all the way down, his feet still firmly planted on the lower one and still gripping the upper one in both hands when he hit the ground.

It seemed like Buddy was still bouncing; still gasping and moaning, trying desperately to pull some air back in his lungs, when his mama reached him and began to lay into him with a switch she had picked up en route. With Buddy still struggling for life, she was ranting at him, "I *told* you not to go climbing no trees!"

At the moment it wasn't funny for I thought Buddy was a goner, either from the fall or from the beating, but, in years since, that picture has given me many a laugh.

Now, let's move on.

I was born at Broadmoor, at home and prematurely, and with some kind of a heart defect, on June 5, 1937. I was what was called, in those days, a blue baby. Today, I would have been born in a hospital and immediately placed in an incubator but in those days it was different. People generally just applied home remedies and then let nature take its course.

I am told that for about three days Aunt Reldie and Grandma, as a substitute for an incubator, sat with me before the open door of a hot oven. I don't know if that made the difference, but I survived, although some of my brothers have since suggested that they might have held me too close to the heat and cooked a part of my brain. When I look back on some of the things I have done in my life, I sometimes think they might be right.

But, setting the jokes aside, Mama has told me that, when it looked like I might not make it, she prayed to God that if He would let me live she would try to raise me in love of Him. I can attest that is one promise she tried her best to keep.

I was four and a half years old at the time of Pearl Harbor, and, even at that age, was able to understand some concept of war. I knew that my Grandmother Reagan lived near a town called Manila. That was in Arkansas and I didn't know there were other places with the same name. So when I heard the adults talking about the Japanese bombing Manila I began to cry; afraid Grandma had been killed or hurt. I was terribly concerned until Mama explained things to me.

Early in the war, a major B-17 training base was established just south of Dyersburg and the big bombers soon became a common sight in our skies. Training bases for other types of aircraft were also established not far away, at Mauldin, Missouri and Blytheville, Arkansas, and there was a naval air station at Millington, Tennessee, near Memphis.

With all those planes in the air, I inevitably became, in my mind, an aviator. Mostly, I flew heavy bombers. I didn't have a uniform but I did have this cap.

In that time and place, we kids spent the most part of every day out of doors and, thus, we all wore some kind of cap to keep our head and ears warm. One kind that was very popular during the war years was a replica of a military flier's helmet. It looked like leather, was fleece-lined, and could be pulled down and fastened with a strap under the chin. And it had goggles. That was important. A pilot's got to have goggles. They attached to the cap with snaps, one in the middle of the front and others on each side of the head. The goggles could be worn down over the eyes but, if the imaginary flier wished, he could unfasten the side snaps, rotate the goggles on the center snap and re-attach them on the sides so that the goggles rode, in dashing fashion, above the eyebrows on the front of the cap.

Well, I had me one of those caps and I wore it all the time; practically slept in it. Years later, when I saw the movie, *Mister Roberts,* I could well identify with the old sea captain when he said to Mr. Roberts, "Mista, you see this heah hat? Ain't nobody gonna come between me and this heah hat!" That hat must have taken me on a thousand imagined missions over Germany and brought me safely home every time.

I dropped many an imaginary bomb but, one day, a real one was nearly dropped on me. I was outside playing with some other kids when I heard the faint hum of engines overhead and looked up and spotted a high-flying B-17. There was, I knew, a practice bombing range near Ridgely, some four miles north and I presumed the bomber was making a run on the range and I paid no further attention to it, that is, until I heard this strange sound that was getting louder and louder. I had learned from a few war movies I had seen what a bomb is supposed to sound like. But the sound I heard was not a piercing whistle. What I heard was a sort of wail, something like wah—wah—WAH—WAH! And then I heard the KA-BOOM! And the ground shook under me and, about a hundred yards away, a large, white plume shot into the air.

Fortunately, as it turned out, this was only a practice bomb filled with sand rather than high explosives but it was still real enough to frighten one small boy who, for the first time, found himself on the receiving end of a bombing raid. Later, I wondered if the airman who dropped this one, and missed the target by a mere four miles, ever made it through bombardier school.

We became so accustomed to seeing the planes, especially the B-17's, many of them flying at only a few hundred feet of altitude, that it almost seemed we were personally acquainted with the individual crews.

There came a day when, out of a bright, cloudless sky, we heard a loud thunderclap and, as we stood, speculating as to its source, there arose out to the west a huge, boiling column of black smoke. Grandpa let me ride with him and we followed the trail of smoke until we reached an open field surrounded by military police and a curious, subdued crowd that stood staring at scattered engines, still burning amid a rubble of smoking metal and a wide swath of blackened earth, and I was overcome by a numb, sad, emptiness inside as I realized I was looking at all that remained of what, a few minutes earlier, was a proudly flying B-17 and its young, still living crew.

After that day my imagined heroic missions had a less glamorous appeal and I began to understand that, in war, even heroes sometime die.

Being a young child, I didn't become closely acquainted with the adults of Broadmoor, other than those in our family, except for one and I have always remembered him. He was an old black man, one who, in today's world, would be viewed as the very picture of an Uncle Tom. He didn't exactly bow and scrape but he always gave deference to any white person.

In that time, it was the common and certain belief among whites that Negroes, under the Devine plan, had their place in society and a black person who knew what his place was, and stayed there, was respected for that. Of course, it was the white man's reading of The Plan that defined the black man's place and that was always a few steps behind any white person and in the back of the bus and at the colored drinking fountains and waiting rooms and in the balcony at the theater.

Alvin was one of those respected for knowing and staying in his place but some of us knew him for another reason. He was a kind and honest man. And he was a friend. He called me "Podnuh."

Many times Lynn and I, both then very young, would be playing outside when Alvin came by our house on his way to work in the fields. He would always stop and have something cheerful to say to us and, before he went on, he would fumble around in his pocket and come out with a piece of hard candy for each of us.

Other times, as I grew older, if I was around the store and Alvin walked up, his face would light up and he would say, "Hey there, podnuh. Don't I owe you a nickel?" And, of course, he would hand me a coin and, for a while, make one little boy rich and happy. In those days that didn't exactly conform to the unwritten code, a black man offering a charitable gift to a white boy, but I was proud then, and would be proud today, to accept the generosity of this kind, gentle man.

Alvin left this earth a long time ago and I'm sure he must now be safely settled in his rightful place and, if there is justice where he is, I am confident he now drinks freely from crystal fountains of his own choice and he rides proudly, with his head held high, in the very front seat of every bus.

It was a sad day for me when our family loaded up all our worldly belongings and left Broadmoor for Arkansas. I remember looking back at Grandma Weaver as she waved us out of sight and thinking I might never see her again. Fortunately, I was wrong about that.

We were poor when we left Broadmoor and poor when we arrived in Arkansas, but there was a difference. On Broadmoor, *everyone* we knew was poor. That was not true in the community we moved into in Arkansas. Many families lived well and ate well and had a car or pickup which they made available to the kids when they were old enough to drive. And they saw that their children had change to jingle in their pockets. Their kids never had to pass up a candy bar or a soft drink or an extra milk at lunch for the reason that they couldn't pay for it.

Many of the people we knew there owned their own farms. The land in that part of the state was laid out in grids, the basic unit being a section, which was one square mile, containing six hundred forty acres. A section was usually further marked off into sixteen quarter-mile squares of forty acres each.

In that era one family could still make a living farming forty acres and they could live well on eighty, especially if they owned the land, as many of the families we knew did.

It was there, in Northeast Arkansas, that I first began to understand that there really are Haves and Have-nots. Let me hasten to say that we had good friends there, many of them among the Haves, and, while we were Have-nots, they did not snub us. It was we, and I in particular, who read so plainly the line between us.

We lived there in Arkansas for five and a half years, aware every day of our station, and with no reason to hope for any betterment. I suspect it was there that, somewhere deep inside me, a seed was sown But, wherever and whenever that happened, the seed would eventually flower into a resolve and determination that would, one day, lift me above the poverty I was born into.

From my early youth until well into maturity, the road I traveled took many turns and I will not try to tell you all of them. I will only give you an overview.

In 1951, we moved to Memphis where I attended schools into the ninth grade but, in 1956, at eighteen, I entered the army, committed for two years, and spent the major part of that time overseas in Germany.

For the trip over, I was to board a troopship, the USNS General Alexander Patch, at New York City. I had never been on, or even seen, a seagoing ship. In fact, I had never seen the ocean before and was a little apprehensive and my tension was not lessened by the news that broke as we prepared to sail. The night before, two ocean liners had collided in the fog off Cape Cod and the Italian, the *Andrea Doria*, was sinking. We, of course, sailed anyway.

By that time I had been in the army a few months and was beginning to understand some of what my older brothers, all veterans, had told me. One had said, "Son, the ways of the military are many and wondrous." And another said, "Make that many and strange."

Listen and see which category the following story falls into.

When I finished basic at Fort Chaffee, Arkansas, I applied for a 12-week course of training as a high speed radio operator but was turned down for the reason, they said, that a man like me, only in for a two years, was not permitted to go to any school longer that eight weeks. When they told me that, I opted for an 8-week field medic course. Then, two weeks into it, they told me I was doing well enough to be bounced up to a more detailed 14-week course for what was called a medical specialist. Maybe I should have pointed out to them that the rules didn't permit that but I decided not to. Let them make their own mistakes. So, considering the preliminary two weeks, I had sixteen weeks of specialized medical training behind me when I shipped out for Germany, eight weeks more than the rules permitted, or so I had been told.

When I arrived in my unit near Stuttgart, I was told by the first sergeant that there was no vacancy for one of my specialty. But first sergeants are well known for their innovative solutions to small problems. Mine, who was then in need of a personnel specialist, promptly shipped me out to a 7-week course in that specialty. But, by the time I finished the school and came back, that need had also been filled.

Well, no problem, no problem! Using his connections, ole sarge hustled me off to another school; this one 13 weeks, to learn to be a medical records specialist.

So it was that I eventually stood once more before the top sergeant, me a soldier now with thirty-six weeks of training in three different specialties; whereas the rules said I was limited to eight weeks in one, and what did the sergeant say to me?

"Hey, Weaver. Glad to have you back. How'd you like to learn to drive a truck?"

With some considerable effort, I fought down a near-hysterical urge to burst into laughter and was able to stammer out that I already knew how to do that.

So that's how I became an army truck driver, but one with useful special skills. See, had my vehicle ever been involved in an accident, I had the training to, on the spot, treat the injured, fill out the necessary medical records, and initiate the appropriate personnel forms transferring us all to the hospital, and do all that before the ambulance arrived.

When I was discharged at the end of 1957, I had, I thought, had enough of the military and I went to work in Memphis for a supermarket chain. Then I got married to Mary Alice Nichols, a girl from Ridgely, and—I guess we should have expected it—Mary soon got pregnant. Realizing I couldn't support a family and pay medical bills on what I earned as a produce clerk, I looked again to the military and I joined the air force.

My darling daughter, Teresa, who would be my only child, was born November 11, 1959, at Blytheville, Arkansas, where I was stationed at the Air Force Base.

I spent the next four years there at Blytheville where, to my good fortune, they allowed me to work in the medical field for which the army had trained me.

It was near the end of that hitch, in 1963, that the seed that had lain dormant inside me for so long, began to grow. I developed a strong desire to advance in the medical field and become a registered nurse. Mary and I talked it over and we decided and agreed that if I could do that it would be worth the three years of near-starvation that would be required of us while I was in school.

I left the air force early that year and we moved to St. Louis where Mary got work and I began my studies at St. Louis City Hospital. The first two years were hard financially; really hard, and I doubt we could have made it without the twenty-five dollars I quietly borrowed from Mama each month. Then, in my final year, I again turned to the military and enrolled in an army program under which they paid me a small salary while I finished the last year of school with the condition that, upon graduation, I would owe them two years of service. So it was that, in late 1966, now an RN, I was commissioned as a second lieutenant in the army.

I paid my two-year debt to the Army while stationed at Ft. Jackson, South Carolina. Then I once more became a civilian. I worked briefly as night nursing supervisor at the Dyersburg hospital while exploring other options and eventually decided to return to active duty with the air force.

I had left the air force some six years earlier as an airman first class on a pay scale that barely allowed me to feed my family. I was returning as a first lieutenant with a salary that now allowed us to subsist with a measure of dignity. But still something drove me on.

As an RN, I was first stationed at Sewart Air Force Base at Smyrna, Tennessee, and was fortunate to be working for a wonderful chief nurse who not only pushed hard for me to go to anesthesia school, but also fast-tracked my promotion to captain. Later, when Sewart was closed, I was sent to Wilford Hall, the USAF hospital at Lackland Air Force Base at San Antonio, Texas.

It was while I was there at Wilford Hall that, with a favorable evaluation from my supervisor, I was accepted in the school of anesthesia. The school was in the same building so I didn't have to move.

The next eighteen and a half months were tough, especially for one like me whose formal education was deficient. I found that, in order to understand the material in some courses, I had to become proficient in other subjects such as algebra, chemistry and other physical sciences. The only way for me to do that was to buy the books and study on my own. Because of this, while my classmates carried five subjects, I might be studying seven or eight.

But in the end I graduated in the top half of my class and (now I'm bragging a little but not ashamed of it) when we took the national qualifying exam for the title and privileges of a Certified Registered Nurse Anesthetist, I not only took first place but was told that my score came close to doubling that of the next highest.

Not bad, I thought, for a farm boy from the poorest family in his community.

As an officer in the air force, I served at Sewart AFB, Smyrna, Tennessee, at Lackland AFB, San Antonio, Texas, at Scott AFB, Bellville, Illinois, and at Webb AFB, Big Spring, Texas. Then, in May, 1975, holding the rank of captain, I left the military for the last time and took up the private practice of anesthesia.

Most of the remainder of my active career I spent at the Henry County Hospital at Paris, Tennessee, where, because of a developing health problem, I finally retired in early 1992.

I still live in Paris, with Norma, my present wife of twenty-three years.

Teresa's mother, who was my first wife, and I were divorced in 1979. She never remarried and, sadly, she died at home at Jackson, Tennessee early this year, 2003.

Let me add one final thing and, if I'm bragging again, I offer no apologies.

I have roughly calculated that, in my career as an anesthetist, counting both military and civilian service, I put more than ten thousand patients to sleep. When my time runs out, you can, if you wish, carve that number on my stone but on the further condition that you add one more line:

"Of that number, he never lost a single one."

Again, I'd say that, for a poor country boy from Broadmoor, that ain't bad.

39

Bueford

I, Bueford, first left Broadmoor when I joined the navy in the spring of 1945 and, while I occasionally returned to visit and maintained friendships there, I never came back to live. After my navy tour I joined Mama and the younger boys in Arkansas and, for one year, farmed as a sharecropper for their landlord, Mr. George Flagg, before moving to Memphis. In early 1952, I again joined the military, this time the air force.

In June of that year, I married Peggy Fussell. While in the air force, we were stationed, first, at Sewart Air Force Base at Smyrna, Tennessee, and, later, at Ardmore Air Force Base in Oklahoma.

When I first left the air force, we returned to Memphis where I worked at the Army General Depot and the Naval Air Station before I was accepted into a program with the Army Ordinance Corps that took us, eventually, to Texarkana, Texas, Hanover, Illinois and Umatilla, Oregon. From Umatilla, I moved to Redstone Arsenal at Huntsville, Alabama, where I remained, working for the Army Missile Command, until retirement.

Let me tell you a little about my travels while I was in the navy. I admit this has nothing to do with Broadmoor except, perhaps, as it illustrates how far it is possible for one to leave it behind, what variety of other adventures the wider world might offer him, how many far more beautiful places he might see, and yet, in the end, find his way back to Broadmoor and know he has come home.

I was on the *Yancey*, AKA 93, a cargo ship. For a while we were stationed on the east coast, where we had a little "banana" run to ports like, Bermuda; San Juan, Puerto Rico; Guantanamo, Cuba; Panama; Norfolk, Virginia, and New York. Then we moved to the west coast where we sailed to Hawaii, Guam, Iwo Jima, New Zealand, and other Pacific islands.

But there was one special cruise.

In 1946, the *Yancey* was selected to participate in Operation Highjump. That was an expedition to the South Pole, led by Admiral Byrd, and it included a dozen or more ships, divided into groups. Among those in our group was another cargo ship, the *Merrick*. The icebreaker with us was the *Northwind*. Aircraft to be used in mapping and exploration were brought in on the carrier, *Phillipine Sea*. There was also a submarine, an oiler and a command ship. The carrier stayed outside the ice and, after landing strips were prepared, launched the planes which flew in to the base we established.

Once we got into the ice pack, the *Northwind,* which was leading the way, was breaking the ice up into large chunks and it got very noisy with those chunks banging against our hull as we pushed through. It also got very cold with ice freezing on the masts and rigging and on the inside of the portion of the steel hulls that were below the water line.

We had a scare on the way in when the whole column, except for the ice breaker, got frozen in and unable to move and the single icebreaker couldn't free us. They had to call in a second ice breaker from one of the other groups to help the *Northwind* break us out. While waiting for it, we were stuck fast in the ice for several days. The commanders were working out an escape plan, just in case. They even sent out some men to explore the feasibility of our walking out across the ice. I suppose the ice would have held us but I never understood where we might walk to. I mean, we had no confidence we might happen upon some cozy little inn where we might rest and sip hot tea and warm our feet before the fire while waiting for rescue. Fortunately, it never came to that and I, for one, felt relieved.

But that wasn't the last of the excitement. One day, after we reached our destination and were tied up in a small, ice-free bay, we had a real scare. The bay was called the Bay of Whales, and the surrounding ice shelf we were tied up to reached, in places, heights of a hundred and fifty feet above the water. The only way in or out of the bay was through a narrow opening, only about a quarter of a mile wide.

One day a very large iceberg which, itself, spanned nearly a quarter of a mile, appeared in the entrance putting our whole group in jeopardy. With the iceberg in the entrance, there was no room for a ship to slip by and escape and if it came on in and caught one or more of our ships up against the ice, it would crush us like a matchbox. We were at the mercy of the iceberg and could only react to its movements, which we couldn't predict.

So that we could maneuver and try to escape it if we had to, we got up steam and sent out parties ready to cast off our lines. But after a while, satisfied, I guess, after having a look at us strange creatures, the iceberg turned around and drifted away and we relaxed.

But these two little adventures were as nothing compared to what we ran into on our way out. The first thing that happened was that the *Merrick* sustained some serious damage before we cleared the ice pack. The *Northwind* could break up the ice but it couldn't pulverize it. It only left it in large chunks. Somehow, some of these chunks got into the *Merrick's* screw (its propeller) and badly damaged both the screw and the ship's rudder. It couldn't steer and couldn't get enough thrust from the screw to move under its own power. The *Northwind* had to take her in tow.

Then, soon after we cleared the ice, a hurricane, with sustained winds over a hundred miles an hour, hit us. The line the *Northwind* had on the *Merrick* snapped and now we were truly in trouble.

The waves churned up by the hurricane were huge. When we were in the troughs, we could see them looming higher than our masts and, when we crested a wave, our screw would come out of the water and the whole ship would vibrate as if it were being shaken in some giant hand. It was bad on the *Yancey* but it was the *Merrick* that was in the greatest danger. Unable to steer, she couldn't maintain a proper bearing in relation to the waves and she was not getting enough thrust from her screw to navigate even if she had been able to steer.

But we couldn't go off and leave our sister ship. Somehow we had to get a tow line on her and, in trying to do that, we had to circle her in the heavy seas and so we began to endure the same punishment as she from the monstrous waves. Our deck cargo; some trucks, small dozers and other vehicles, began to break loose. Some went over the side and some were saved when deck crews, fighting to keep themselves from being washed away by the huge waves breaking over our decks, were able to strengthen their tie-downs. Down in the holds, other things began to break loose, including some large cases of dynamite. Each bouncing, rolling crate or item of cargo had to be tackled and wrestled into position and re-secured, and this had to be done while every other loose thing was rolling and tumbling and becoming a potentially deadly missile ready to crush any sailor caught in its path. And we struggled to do this in the dim-lit hold of a ship that was pitching violently end to end and rolling 90 degrees from side to side!

In my later years there have been other times when I knew this old country boy was a long way from Broadmoor but never have I so passionately yearned to feel its solid gumbo beneath my feet as I did on that long, wet, freezing night of terror in that raging sea!

But we survived the storm and with, to my knowledge, no loss of life. I don't know if it was skilled seamanship that brought us through or if it was Someone Else whose name I heard mentioned a few times that night who deserves the credit. But, at last, we got our line on the *Merrick,* the storm passed, and, over the next several days, we towed her into Port Chalmers on New Zealand's South Island where we stayed for a week or ten days.

We had been to New Zealand before, but always to the more industrialized North Island. We enjoyed the city of Dunedin and some of us took bus trips into the countryside. Here there were beautiful, rolling hills where they farmed and raised sheep and had small towns with little tea shops and I will always remember that tranquil place of good food, friendly people and lovely pastoral views.

We were a little sad when we left New Zealand behind, most of us knowing we would never return, but then our next stop was Samoa. Let me tell you about Samoa.

We anchored off the island of Tutuila in American Samoa near the little village of Pago Pago, which, for reasons I don't know, is pronounced Pango Pango. We found the natives to be very friendly. They lived in little thatch buildings with sides that could be rolled up to let the breezes blow through. Their houses were within a short distance of the ocean with sharp mountains rising close behind them.

The Samoans generally wore a garment called a lava lava which was something like a bed sheet wrapped around their waist and tucked in to secure it. It was a style of dress unfamiliar to us but the thing that first attracted our attention was not what they wore below the waist but what they wore above. And that was nothing. Men, women, children, everybody, went topless. The Samoans were a handsome race and the young girls were particularly lovely. Few of us had ever seen such beauty (let me be honest; I mean beauties) before.

I believe, in general, we sailors were somewhat surprised to find we could walk among and mingle with so many bare breasted girls and find there was no sense of shyness or discomfort on either side. The girls' unabashed nudity was, we soon recognized, not intended to tempt or tease us but was a reflection of their culture and was, for them, a natural state. We, at least most of us, respected that and treated these lovely girls the same as we would those of any other society.

I will tell you of one other memory of the Samoan people. When the *Yancey* sailed from Samoa, we brought with us a young person of royalty. We understood he was a king. He proved to be a nice and friendly person (as all Samoans were) and was en route to Hawaii where he would enter the university there. When he debarked in Honolulu we had to chuckle as he walked, barefooted but confidently, away from the ship. In view of the customs we had observed on his home island, we speculated that he had probably never owned a pair of shoes.

I never knew why, upon leaving the cold Antarctic, our commanders granted us those stops in two such beautiful places as New Zealand and Samoa but I will be forever grateful that they did.

When, at last, my navy hitch was up, I was glad to be going home but I still carry with me some good memories of the old *Yancey* and I remember the last time I saw her. She was steaming under the San Francisco Bay Bridge outbound and on her way to Alaska and, for just a moment there, I admit I was thinking, "Boy, I'd like to make that cruise. I've never been to Alaska."

I realize that, by now, you may have had quite enough of my private history but there is a part of me you don't yet know about and I am bound to confess.

I am a Baptist preacher.

I have been for nearly forty years. And, if you know anything about Baptist preachers, you know that, once one of us has the pulpit, he doesn't easily give it up. So now I'm going to preach to you a little bit. However, I promise, this time, I will be brief.

The first thing I will do is cut the levity for I am dead serious about my faith and how it came to me and what I have done with it.

While I didn't acknowledge it then, I believe I first heard God speak to me when I was a young sailor walking alone on the crowded streets of New York City. That was the first time I heard him but he might have spoken to me before when I wasn't listening.

Anyway, on that occasion, I clearly heard a voice calling my name, "Bueford...Bueford." It was my immediate thought that it must be someone who knew me from home, for, to all my shipmates, I was known as Jim or just "Weaver." But, when I turned and searched the faces in the throng, I saw no one I recognized. I walked on but I was troubled. The voice had come so clear and there was something that told me it was real, and who it was, but I didn't accept that at the time. I concluded the voice had flowed from the wishful mind of a lonely sailor a long way from home. I dismissed the voice but I remembered it.

Then, some sixteen years later, I heard the voice again and this time there was no mistaking who spoke to me. The local pastor had come to visit and, while we talked, I heard The Voice and it reminded me of a passage in Luke. It was after the risen Lord had revealed himself to the disciples from Emmaus and, "They said one to another, did not our heart burn within us, while he talked with us by the way, and while he opened to us the scriptures?"

That night I went to bed a Christian.

Nearly two years later the voice again came to me and told me to go and preach. Again, like the youth on that New York city street, I convinced myself it was my imagination. But The Voice did not let me go. So I talked to my pastor. That was on a Wednesday night and he said, "All right. You preach next Sunday and Sunday night."

Well, I was a little scared, thinking that maybe me and the Lord might be rushing things a bit. I still remember that I chose the text for my first sermon from the book of Revelations, Chapter 3, verses 14–19, which says, in part, (verse 17) "Because thou sayest: I am rich and increased with goods, and have need of nothing: and knowest not that thou art wretched, and miserable, and poor, and blind, and naked."

Well, that last part pretty well described me when I stood and faced that congregation for the first time. But, somehow we, that is me and the Lord, got through it and I knew I had correctly heard the call.

From then until I retired, I worked full time and preached part time, always in small churches; all on and around Brindlee Mountain in Northern Alabama. I came off the bench a lot, filling in where they had no regular pastor. At last count, I had pastored at least nine churches. But let me explain. I was never asked *to leave* a church but to *come to* a different one.

I believe I served the Lord's purpose and I made a lot of life-long friends while doing it. Along the way I had a few frustrations but a far greater number of inspiring moments. I remember the two young twin girls I baptized at the same time and the seventy-five year old man. And there was the elderly lady who had been baptized as a child but who had always wanted to do it again when she could know and feel what was happening to her. When it was done, the joy this simple but deeply significant ceremony brought to her shone brightly on her face.

I remember the time I was to preach a funeral at a small, country church and we learned, just as we were to leave the funeral home for the church, that the singers the family thought were arranged for would not be there. Dismayed and with no idea what I was going to do or say, I arrived with the procession at the church. And there, as I dismounted, I was met by a stranger who explained he was from another congregation and had come and brought with him a group of singers. He said they had been concerned and wanted to be there "Just in case."

I shouldn't have been surprised for that's the way country people are: anticipating a neighbor's need and ready to fill it; and not waiting to be asked. I don't think I ever participated in a more beautiful funeral service.

There are many more things I could tell you about my career as a preacher but I will mention only two of them and the memory of these two I will carry with me always. They are the times I delivered the funeral addresses for my brother, Vernon, and for Gene's wife, Joann. People have since asked me how I was able to do it and I usually put their question aside without an answer. But I will tell you.

During other services, I have often said to surviving family that we are gathered, not to mourn, but to celebrate the life that has ended and then, later, I have asked myself if that is really true or just words intended to comfort. But now I know and I say this to you, and I say it especially to Vernon and Joann. When I say those words I speak the truth. We who remain will always miss you and mourn your passing but our sadness is far exceeded by the memories you leave with us of all the good times.

Now, that ends my sermon for the day.

As I believe you will see, I have had a better life than I probably deserve. I have had loving family and faithful friends and, in my time and travels, with the navy and otherwise, I have seen a few sights but the most beautiful and inspiring of all I have seen are my own, private Seven Wonders of the World; the faces of the seven beautiful children Peg and I brought into this world, Lynn, Myra, Belinda, Jimmy, Susie, Sharon and David.

Thank you, Lord.

40

The Beginning of the End

Now, I am afraid I have again let my mind stray from my subject, which is Broadmoor. Let me return.

With the beginning of World War Two, Broadmoor began a slide toward its inevitable end. It wasn't noticed; not then, not for years even, but the seeds were sown and, over time, they would germinate.

Either through military service or the magnet of city jobs, the young men who might have led Broadmoor into the future were taken away and exposed to new and broader horizons. They learned of things like indoor plumbing, electric lights, regular showers and a weekly pay check and they began to look toward goals other than the hope, maybe next year, of having their own mule team.

At the same time a boom of mechanization was building. A single man on a John Deere could do the work of ten mule teams and do it better and cheaper. One-family, one-mule-team, farms no longer made sense. Whereas a hundred acres was once a substantial farm, a thousand was now too small. These changes took a few years to fully develop but there came a time that the need for a man with a cotton sack, a plow or a hoe was no more.

41

The Tornado

In the spring of 1952, as if she had become impatient and anxious to hurry the ending along, Mother Nature sent a messenger. The tornado. By that time, the Weaver family had been gone from Broadmoor for several years but Sue Kennedy (now Sue Inlow), about fourteen at that time, still lived there with her family in quarters above the store. Sue remembers and this is how she recently described that day.

> March 21 1952, was a very eerie day. Coming home from school, I remember telling Rachel (Sue's mother's baby sister) that the weather seemed weird and I sure hoped we would not have a stormy night. Papa Nale (her grandfather, Ed Nale) had a storm house and, believe me, when storms came, we went to the storm house. But spending nights in the storm house is another story.
>
> That evening late, my daddy and mother and Metha and myself went to Ridgely to get the windshield wipers on the car fixed. They were worn and Mother had had trouble getting home from work, due to the heavy rain. It was raining very hard and we visited with friends, Mary and Orville Barber, in Ridgely. It was raining very hard; thundering and lightning continuously. I remember Daddy standing on the Barbers' front porch, looking toward Broadmoor and saying he was afraid Broadmoor was having a very bad storm.
>
> Just as soon as we could get to our car, we headed home. Lightning was still very bad.
>
> Bill and Eloise Lay and their small son, Billy, lived in the first house as you cross the Dyer County line, coming into Broadmoor from Ridgely and when we got to where the house should have been the house was not there, not even a plank, and we saw their car was blown into the ditch. Driving on slowly, we noticed that the next house, Mr. Dudley's, was blown off the blocks and their barn roof was caved in. We saw some flashlights shining where the family was attempting to get their cattle out of the damaged barn.
>
> The Wallace Dudley house (Wallace was Mr. Dudley's son) was severely damaged.
>
> As we arrived at the store, (where we lived upstairs) we saw a lady standing on the front porch. The electricity was off but we could see by the continuous

lightning and Daddy recognized her as his sister, my Aunt Lillie. He asked if she and her family were all right and she said they were except they no longer had a house. Daddy told her to stay there while we drove over to check on my mother's parents and Rachel. We found them in the storm house and they were okay. Their house was damaged some but livable.

By the time we drove back to the store It seemed all the Broadmoor families had gathered there. We learned that most of their homes were destroyed or badly damaged.

When a count was made, we thought all the families were accounted for except Mr. Bill and Mrs. Eloise Lay and their little boy, Billy, and the men were preparing to go look for them. We later found another couple was missing.

Daddy unlocked the store and got flashlights and batteries and gave one to each man and they went out into the muddy fields and began to search. I remember it was so eerie and scary, watching from the store, with destruction all around; and seeing all the flashlights shining out in that field and knowing what they were looking for but not knowing what they would find.

After an hour or two the men came back to the store and told us they had found Bill and Eloise's bodies but that they did not find their son. It was some time before they found the little boy and he was alive. He had been blown up under their car and suffered only a broken nose. His mother had wrapped him in a bed quilt and that probably saved him.

Some time later they found the bodies of the other couple (They were Bonnie and George Minnick. Bonnie was Mr. Rube Cherry's granddaughter.) They had been blown into a field near Mr. Cherry's house. What made the girl's death more tragic was that she was expecting a baby that was due, some said, that very night.

Two days later I attended both families' funerals on the same day. That was a very sad day for the Broadmoor community.

The store building was badly damaged. The roof was blown off and all our clothes and the bed clothing were soaked. The Broadmoor Church of Christ that was directly across the highway was completely destroyed.

Our friend, Verbal Gore of Ridgely owned a dry cleaning business. He came the next day and got all our clothes and bed linens and cleaned them and returned them the following day.

Beginning the next morning, and for the next two days, we had bumper to bumper traffic with people who had heard about the storm and came to see.

Clean up was a very sad time.

Mr. and Mrs. Dan Lay, his aunt and uncle, took little Billy Lay and raised him and he is now married and lives somewhere in Texas. I haven't seen him in several years.

With the help of other congregations sending money, the Broadmoor Church of Christ was rebuilt and they, even now, continue to have weekly services there with an average of twenty to thirty people from other close by communities attending.

I will never forget that night. I am still very much afraid of any storm. When I hear we are having a tornado watch or warning, I head for my basement. Any storm we have when the lightning is bad, I always think of the tornado at Broadmoor. I can still see all the flashlights shining in the fields looking for the two couples.

I will never forget that night.

The storm was more or less the beginning of families moving away from Broadmoor, looking for employment elsewhere. After the storm, most of the houses standing were not really structurally safe. At the time of the tornado, Broadmoor had at least twenty families. Now one person does all the farming and no one lives on the land.

I still call Broadmoor home and will always cherish the good memories.

That was Sue's account of the tornado and its effects.

42

Finality

The exodus that had begun before the storm accelerated afterward. One by one the old families moved away and slowly the portrait of Broadmoor as a community faded until, where once there was color and life and form, only a blank and barren canvas remained.

To accommodate bigger and faster agricultural machines, the virgin forests we roamed in our youth were slashed and burned with no effort even made to harvest the timber. The dozens of tenant houses that once rang with children's laughter were razed. Where before there had been smaller, identifiable, plots of land like the Henderson place, the Johnson's, the Weaver farms and others, there remained but one broad field, now swept clean of all character.

It was all gone. Broadmoor had succumbed to the wounds of progress. It had died a lingering death, denied even the solace of a single remaining mourner to shed a tear at its passing.

43

Other Goodbyes

Grandpa Weaver and Grandma are long gone, as are Uncle Cheat and Aunt Reldie. Daddy is gone and so is Dirk.

Many of our Broadmoor friends have left us; most of the older ones long ago, of course. Others that we know of include Mister Sam and Miss Pearl Fussell and their son, Bo; Waltie Kennedy and his daughter, Metha; both J.C. and Gerald Buchanan, Junior Wolf and Perchworthy and probably others of whom I am unaware.

And gone, far too soon, is the crooked grin and tousled hair and irrepressible good humor of every one's favorite friend, Joe Henderson.

Before we leave here, I feel compelled to offer some manner of farewell to Daddy. But, before I do that, let me correct an omission. Thus far, I have told you nothing of the girl who ran away with Daddy nor of the family they later raised together.

We believe the girl, Katherine, was as innocent as we were when she was led into that affair by a much older man. We have never settled any blame upon her and we have always counted the four fine children they raised, Linda, Venita, Mercedes and John as our sisters and brother, which, in fact, they are, and we love them.

Any blame that is to be assessed must rest on Daddy and on him alone. And, while it is true he did us a grave wrong when he deserted Mama and us kids, Mama always taught us, and we later saw she was right, that we would only harm ourselves by continuing to harbor ill will toward him and we have not done so.

Daddy made a mistake, a bad mistake, but, for that, I believe he has, over the years, in some manner or form, paid a cost.

In another writing we, as his sons, addressed this matter and said it this way.

What can we say about Daddy?

He gave us life. He showed us love. He gave us lessons in compassion for others. He demonstrated to us the value of hard work and industry and planning and execution of plans. He taught us that what one can envision he can do, and he can do it with his own hands.

But he also showed us how the world appears when viewed from the pit of despair.

And we said:

Somewhere beyond this place, we believe, there lies a river and, for those who cross it, its waters will rinse the tears from our eyes and cleanse our soul of the stain of our transgressions and wash away all memory of pain.

In our hearts, Daddy, we have erased old debts and have closed the book and now wish only this for you:

Cross the river safely. Receive from its coolness absolution and in some far meadow find you peace and gentle sleep and let us begin anew in the morning.

44

One Final Fling

It was the fall of 1953. Gene and Lynn were young and free as the wind. Gene had, that summer, completed his time with the army and was still luxuriating in release from its daily discipline. Career plans were far from his mind. Lynn, then just eighteen, was having much too much fun to look beyond tomorrow. The boys were tied to, and responsible for, nothing and no one and the wonder of the season was upon them. Blue skies, idyllic days and an open door to all that was good in the world called irresistibly to them. They went down to Broadmoor for a weekend visit with Cheat and Reldie and stayed the whole season.

Days they picked cotton and evenings they met with all that remained of Broadmoor youth and just let the world roll by. Except for them, the only boys left were Bo, Perchworthy, and Harvey and Joe Henderson and the only girls were Marcene and Sharon Robinson and the Kennedy girls, Metha and Sue. (And, yes, Sue still had them eyes and the lilting laugh.) Sharon was Marcene's little sister and, because she spent a lot of time sitting on their porch, singing as she rocked in the porch swing, they called her "Tweety Bird."

Evenings, after they had shed the dust of the fields, the boys would usually drive up to Ridgely, pick up a twelve-pack, and come back to Broadmoor and park on the local equivalent of the village green; a grassy, shaded area across the highway from the store and beside the Robinson girls' house. There the boys would pop a top or two, lounge around and talk some and laugh a lot and, usually, the girls would come out and join them.

They and the girls had known each other all their lives and the boys could talk as frankly and easily with the girls as with each other, but they weren't thought of as girlfriends. If, as sometimes happened, the boys got romance in their minds, they would leave those lovely girls behind and go out huntin' *women!*

However, as things have been known to happen between boys and girls, an exception to this rule began to grow. Glances between Bo and Marcene were somehow subtly changed and the others sensed something was beginning to develop there. Later on, in fact, Bo and Marcene were married. But, for that season, the rest of them retained their immunity to whatever virus it is that causes such things. They weren't boys and girls competing for each others' attentions, they were just a bunch of buddies, lost in the freedom of youth.

But then, sadly, time caught up with them; the weather changed; all the cotton was picked; the village green faded to its winter shade of gray and duty eventually called and Gene and Lynn had to find real work.

But they had, and will always remember, that final, glorious season when Broadmoor still lived and time flowed slowly and care existed only in some other world.

45

Requiem

Now, we have come to the end of our story and once again, as we did in our long ago youth, and as we did on that chill October day we describe at the beginning, my brothers and I say goodbye to Broadmoor. Our coming here has been a journey not only of nostalgia but also one of exploration. We came not only seeking memories but also in a quest for the origins of the undeniable call that brought us back here.

Most of our lives we have spent elsewhere. In other places we put down roots and pursued careers and raised families and made many faithful friends. And along the way we have found happiness. So why, of all the places we have dwelt, is it Broadmoor that most clearly speaks to us of home?

I think, perhaps, we now know the answer. Broadmoor is the place we were first tested as a family and, with no source of help but each other, we met the test and learned we could survive and that knowledge made us strong.

As we matured and life led us away on our individual paths, the image of Broadmoor went with us as a symbol of permanence on which we could depend. At Broadmoor we were safe and free from fear. It was a time of innocence, a time when the threat of a wider world had yet to be perceived. Broadmoor was things promised, as constant as the mother's heartbeat that soothes the sleeping child. It was springtime fields that spoke of new beginnings and autumn's certainty of things harvested and stored away. It was warm fires and loving arms shielding against winter's winds and it was a young boy's refuge from outbound paths that, in time, would inevitably take him away.

And now, as the days or our time grow short, it is here, to this place, to the Broadmoor of our youth, that we return in our hearts and minds and memory and we find here sanctuary and peace and comfort and safety and certitude. And we believe we know, now, what moved the hand that wrote the few words that mark a stone now standing on a windswept hill in far off Samoa. These words, on the tomb of the adventurer, writer and poet, Robert Lewis Stephenson, could well, when the time comes, be ours.

> Under the wide and starry sky
>   Dig the grave and let me lie:
> Glad did I live and gladly die,
>   And I laid me down with a will.
>
> This be the verse you 'grave for me:
>   *Here he lies where he long'd to be;*
> *Home is the sailor, home from the sea*
>   *And the hunter home from the hill.*

0-595-29127-9